A Collection of
Inspiring Calligraphy Poems

A Treasure Trove of Calligraphy Poems for Every Occasion
is a resource you can use again and again. There are so many uses for the
poems in this book. Many can be hand-colored or personalized, and many are
pre-matted with a digital matte, and all will fit a standard 8x10 frame.

In addition, each individual poem can be purchased as a PDF for multiple uses at:

PDFcalligraphy.com

Create a card, use in a scrap book, frame for a friend or
hang on your own wall as a source of inspiration.

You will find a variety of uses for celebrating these Special Occasions:

Adoption	Bridal Shower	Friendship	Mother's Day	Thank You
Anniversary	Christmas	Funeral/Bereavement	Nurse's Day	Thanksgiving
Baby Shower	Easter	Graduation	Retirement	Valentine's Day
Baptism	Encouragement	Grandparent's Day	Scripture/Inspiration	Wedding
Birthday	Father's Day	House Welcome	Teacher Appreciation	

A Treasure Trove of Calligraphy Poems for Every Occasion
by Mary Kay Brewster
Copyright © 2018 Mary Kay Brewster, all rights reserved.
For ancillary rights information: Mary Kay Brewster, pdfcalligraphy@aol.com
No part of this publication may be reproduced, stored in a retrieval system, or transmitted
in any form by means, electronic, mechanical, photocopying, recording, or otherwise
without the prior written permission of the author.

FIRST EDITION 2018

Published by Mary Kay Brewster, Bloomington, IL | www.pdfcalligraphy.com
Cover & Book Design, Rae Ella House | raehouse.com
ISBN 978-1-7324738-0-5
Printed and bound in the United States of America

Mary Kay Brewster

Which Came First, Poetry or Calligraphy? — For Mary Kay Brewster, calligraphy was the first form of art she learned from her high school art teacher, Jim Smith, at Henry Clay HS, Lexington, KY. She first learned an Old English style of calligraphy and did her first manuscript, taken from Proverbs 3, which she presented to her English teacher, Carol Rambo, whom she greatly admired. Later, while attending Bob Jones University as an Art Education Major, she mastered the calligraphy style 'Chancery Cursive' from Katherine Bell. From this, she was hooked on the art of calligraphy.

After creating several calligraphy pieces for her family and friends as gifts, her husband Kevin pointed to a calligraphy art display in the Hickory Point Mall in Decatur, IL — "You could do that!" he said. That was all the motivation and inspiration she needed. She pulled out her pen and ink supplies and went to work. In a few short weeks, she had 13 various pieces to display, and started booking several arts and craft shows for her and her husband to display her work.

It didn't take long to see the need for various poems for special occasions and gift-giving needs. To this end, she wrote poems to meet the requests they would receive from admirers. After 30 years of writing poems and doing calligraphy, it seemed only logical to put together *A Treasure Trove of Calligraphy Poems,* a beautiful, published collection of calligraphy poems for others to share. Some of Mary Kay's favorite poems about God's love and power are the ones she loves to call "Downloads from Heaven". It is her prayer that the poems in this book will touch hearts while offering you a treasure trove of gift giving.

It is only fitting that Mary Kay dedicates this book to her husband Kevin and her six children, Adam, Jason, Wesley, Kaylee, Melody, and Emily from which many of her poems were inspired as she wrote about the many treasures of family and the experiences they shared together.

———————

"Mary Kay also wishes to thank her sister, Rae Ella House, an artist, designer, and marketing specialist in Lexington, KY, for creating the pages and cover of this book, and for helping to make this publication a reality."

TABLE *of* CONTENTS

Unselfish Love

There is no greater love on earth than
the unselfish love of a mother who bears a child
she cannot keep and gives him to another.

She could have taken his life away.
Some say it is her right.
But deep inside she knew this child
should have his chance at life.

Oh, what a special mother
who will deal with grief and pain
so her child can have a better life;
her sacrifice was not in vain.

For someday when her child is grown
and he asks of his legacy,
he'll learn of her unselfish love
and be as proud as he can be.

Mary Kay Brewster

PDFCalligraphy.com

Though you're not
flesh of my flesh
nor bone of my bone,
I proudly consider
you to be my own.
And though you
did not grow under
my heart, within
it you managed to
grow from the start.

PDFCalligraphy.com

CATEGORY: **ADOPTION**   TITLE: **THOUGH YOU'RE NOT** *(can be personalized)*

FITS 8 X 10 FRAME | FOR FUTURE USE, A PRINTABLE PDF CAN BE PURCHASED AT **PDFCALLIGRAPHY.COM**   2

Handpicked

We marvel at how God must have known
to reach down and handpick us,
to love and care for this dear child
and to our home entrust.

He's given us this precious child
that He picked with special care,
for us to raise and guide through life:
what joy we have to share!

We'll share how we all are adopted
to be children of the King.
God adopted us to be His own,
and now this gift we bring.

We give this child right back to You.
We bring him to Your throne.
We dedicate this chosen child,
for we know he is Your own.

We'll care for him in every way;
we'll teach him of Your love.
He's not only adopted on this earth,
he's adopted from above.

Mary Kay Brewster

PDFCalligraphy.com

CUT ALONG DOTTED LINE

Handpicked

We marvel at how God must have known
to reach down and handpick us,
to love and care for this dear child
and to our home entrust.

He's given us this precious child
that He picked with special care,
for us to raise and guide through life:
what joy we have to share!

We'll share how we all are adopted
to be children of the King.
God adopted us to be His own,
and now this gift we bring.

We give this child right back to You.
We bring her to Your throne.
We dedicate this chosen child,
for we know she is Your own.

We'll care for her in every way;
we'll teach her of Your love.
She's not only adopted on this earth,
she's adopted from above.

Mary Kay Brewster

PDFCalligraphy.com

CATEGORY: **ADOPTION**   TITLE: **HANDPICKED (FOR GIRL)**

FITS 8 X 10 FRAME | FOR FUTURE USE, A PRINTABLE PDF CAN BE PURCHASED AT **PDFCALLIGRAPHY.COM**   4

I'm Adopted

I know I am adopted. My parents told me so.
They care for me and love me. That's all I need to know.

But still I have to wonder who brought me to this earth.
Oh, how I'd like to thank her for deciding to give birth.

I know she must have wrestled with pain that hurt so deep.
She gave birth to a little baby she knew she could not keep.

I'd be selfish to ever imagine that she gave me up in vain.
I know deep down inside my heart she did it for my gain.

I've gained two caring parents that have raised me as their own.
I'm thankful for the love and care
that through the years they've shown.

And if I ever have a chance to meet my real birth mother,
I'd thank her for the choice she made
and I'd tell her that I admire her.

Mary Kay Brewster

PDFCalligraphy.com

CATEGORY: **ADOPTION**   TITLE: **I'M ADOPTED**

FITS 8 X 10 FRAME | FOR FUTURE USE, A PRINTABLE PDF CAN BE PURCHASED AT **PDFCALLIGRAPHY.COM**   5

Our Anniversary

This is a celebration day
to look back and reflect
On the memories we've created
since that special day we met.

The years only seem like days...
and the days like only minutes.
Our love makes time stand still,
yet there's an eternity to share it.

So let's cherish every moment
for the treasure that it holds,
And hold on to one another
as we watch our love unfold.

Mary Kay Brewster ©96

PDFCalligraphy.com

On This Your Day

On this your anniversary day,
       as you celebrate your love,
Reflect upon the years you've spent
       and all the things you've done.

The years all seem to blend into one
as your love has stood time's test.
       Each day is as if you've just begun
as you give each other your best

Look back and cherish the love you've shared
       and anticipate memories to come
For your love will last eternally
       as your hearts entwine as one.

Mary Kay Brewster©96

CATEGORY: ANNIVERSARY   TITLE: **ON THIS YOUR DAY**

FITS 8 X 10 FRAME | FOR FUTURE USE, A PRINTABLE PDF CAN BE PURCHASED AT **PDFCALLIGRAPHY.COM**   **7**

Time For Us

Oh how I wish that you and I
could find a quiet place.
We could let our hearts entwine
and adopt a slower pace.

Our love is such a precious thing
and time is hard to find.
Wouldn't it be wonderful
to leave our cares behind.

So let us not forget my dear,
midst the routine and the fuss,
To celebrate our special love
and find some time for us.

—M.K. Brewster © 96   PDFCalligraphy.com

It doesn't matter
where you go in life...
what you do... or how much you have...
It's who you have beside you.

PDFCalligraphy.com

CATEGORY: **ANNIVERSARY**   TITLE: **IT DOESN'T MATTER** *(can be personalized)*

FITS 8 X 10 FRAME | FOR FUTURE USE, A PRINTABLE PDF CAN BE PURCHASED AT **PDFCALLIGRAPHY.COM**   9

Aunts

Aunts are special people—
  they have a unique way
Of reminding you of mom or dad
  in all they do or say.

She may be your mom's sister;
  perhaps your dad's her brother.
But whatever the relationship
  she's a special surrogate mother.

She shares her love in many ways
  with a special kind of kinship.
But most of all she has a way
  of creating special friendships.

—Mary Kay Brewster
© 96

PDFCalligraphy.com

CATEGORY: **AUNTS**   TITLE: **AUNTS** *(like a surrogate mother)*

FITS 8 X 10 FRAME | FOR FUTURE USE, A PRINTABLE PDF CAN BE PURCHASED AT **PDFCALLIGRAPHY.COM**

To My Aunt

Thank you for being my very best friend,
for patiently sharing life's ups and downs.
For giving your time to listen and care,
your understanding spirit is always there.

You are the sunshine of all my glad days
the rainbow that brightens all my sad days.
When life offers thorns you're the rose among them.
No wonder I deem you my very best friend

No words can express my love and affection
as I humbly offer my appreciation
You are as good as a friend can be—
You are God's special gift to me.

PDFCalligraphy.com

CATEGORY: **AUNTS** TITLE: **TO MY AUNT**

FITS 8 X 10 FRAME | FOR FUTURE USE, A PRINTABLE PDF CAN BE PURCHASED AT **PDFCALLIGRAPHY.COM** 11

TINY FOOTPRINTS

Here are your tiny footprints,
as tiny as can be.
Where ever they will take you
is but a mystery.
You're just a tiny baby
who needs a guiding hand;
A hand to gently lead you
and help you understand.
To lead you on the path of life,
to solve its mysteries.
To help you understand your place,
to be all that you can be.
So grow now tiny footprints,
too soon you'll be full grown.
You have a wondrous path to trod,
you need not go alone.
I'll be there right beside you,
guiding all the while.
For you see I love you so,
you are my precious child.

Mary Kay Brewster

MB©'93

PDFCalligraphy.com

CATEGORY: **BABY**   TITLE: **TINY FOOTPRINTS** (add footprints & personalize balloons)

Our Baby Boy

You are our precious little boy;
a miraculous dream come true.
You showed up in our lives one day.
We knew God gave us you.
What a handsome little boy you are,
with delicate hands and feet.
We marvel at how you could be
so precious and so sweet.
Our little angel was sent to us,
no doubt, from heaven above,
to bring us joy and happiness:
and fill our hearts with love.
So, grow now precious baby boy;
too soon you'll be full grown.
You have a wondrous path ahead,
you need not go alone.
We'll be there right beside you,
guiding you all the while.
For you see, we love you so,
you are our precious child.

~Mary Kay Brewster

PDFCalligraphy.com

Our Baby Girl

You are our precious little girl;
a miraculous dream come true.
You showed up in our lives one day.
We knew God gave us you.
What a beautiful little girl you are,
with delicate hands and feet.
We marvel at how you could be
so precious and so sweet.
Our little angel was sent to us,
no doubt, from heaven above,
to bring us joy and happiness
and fill our hearts with love.
So, grow now precious baby girl,
too soon you'll be full grown.
You have a wondrous path ahead,
you need not go alone.
We'll be there right beside you,
guiding you all the while.
For you see, we love you so,
you are our precious child.

~Mary Kay Brewster

PDFCalligraphy.com

CUT ALONG DOTTED LINE

CATEGORY: **BABY**   TITLE: **OUR BABY GIRL**

FITS 8 X 10 FRAME | FOR FUTURE USE, A PRINTABLE PDF CAN BE PURCHASED AT **PDFCALLIGRAPHY.COM**   14

CATEGORY: **BATHROOM**   TITLE: **MY OTHER BATHROOM** *(personalize sign)*

FITS 8 X 10 FRAME | FOR FUTURE USE, A PRINTABLE PDF CAN BE PURCHASED AT **PDFCALLIGRAPHY.COM**   15

CATEGORY: **BATHROOM**   TITLE: **BATHTUB BEARS 2** *(personalize towels)*

FITS 8 X 10 FRAME | FOR FUTURE USE, A PRINTABLE PDF CAN BE PURCHASED AT **PDFCALLIGRAPHY.COM**   16

CATEGORY: **BATHROOM**   TITLE: **BATHTUB BEARS 3** *(personalize towels)*

FITS 8 X 10 FRAME | FOR FUTURE USE, A PRINTABLE PDF CAN BE PURCHASED AT **PDFCALLIGRAPHY.COM**   17

CATEGORY: **BATHROOM**   TITLE: **BATHTUB BEARS 4** *(personalize towels)*

FITS 8 X 10 FRAME | FOR FUTURE USE, A PRINTABLE PDF CAN BE PURCHASED AT **PDFCALLIGRAPHY.COM**

Scrub a dub dub...

PDFCalligraphy.com

CATEGORY: **BATHROOM**   TITLE: **BATHTUB BEARS 5** *(personalize towels)*

FITS 8 X 10 FRAME | FOR FUTURE USE, A PRINTABLE PDF CAN BE PURCHASED AT **PDFCALLIGRAPHY.COM**   19

CATEGORY: **BATHROOM**   TITLE: **BATHTUB BEARS 6** *(personalize towels)*

FITS 8 X 10 FRAME | FOR FUTURE USE, A PRINTABLE PDF CAN BE PURCHASED AT **PDFCALLIGRAPHY.COM**   20

Bath Rules

Occupancy of more than forty persons at a time is prohibited. All bathers please refrain from eating the soap. If there is a ring in the tub please answer it. Guest towels are to be used by guests. Non-guests please dry hands on clothes. Singing in the shower is permitted but dancing is frowned upon.

Please remove rubber ducky after each bath.

PDFCalligraphy.com

CATEGORY: **BATHROOM**   TITLE: **BATH RULES 2** *(add hair & personalize towels)*

FITS 8 X 10 FRAME | FOR FUTURE USE, A PRINTABLE PDF CAN BE PURCHASED AT **PDFCALLIGRAPHY.COM**   21

Bath Rules

Occupancy of more than forty persons at a time is prohibited. All bathers please refrain from eating the soap. If there is a ring in the tub please answer it. Guest towels are to be used by guests. Non-guests please dry hands on clothes. Singing in the shower is permitted but dancing is frowned upon. Please remove rubber ducky after each bath.

PDFCalligraphy.com

CATEGORY: **BATHROOM**   TITLE: **BATH RULES 3** *(add hair & personalize towels)*

FITS 8 X 10 FRAME | FOR FUTURE USE, A PRINTABLE PDF CAN BE PURCHASED AT **PDFCALLIGRAPHY.COM**   22

Bath Rules

Occupancy of more than forty persons at a time is prohibited. All bathers please refrain from eating the soap. If there is a ring in the tub please answer it. Guest towels are to be used by guests. Non-guests please dry hands on clothes. Singing in the shower is permitted but dancing is frowned upon. Please remove rubber ducky after each bath.

PDFCalligraphy.com

CATEGORY: **BATHROOM**   TITLE: **BATH RULES 4** (add hair & personalize towels)

FITS 8 X 10 FRAME | FOR FUTURE USE, A PRINTABLE PDF CAN BE PURCHASED AT **PDFCALLIGRAPHY.COM**   23

Bath Rules

Occupancy of more than forty persons at a time is prohibited. All bathers please refrain from eating the soap. If there is a ring in the tub please answer it. Guest towels are to be used by guests. Non-guests please dry hands on clothes. Singing in the shower is permitted but dancing is frowned upon.

Please remove rubber ducky after each bath.

PDFCalligraphy.com

CATEGORY: **BATHROOM**   TITLE: **BATH RULES 5** *(add hair & personalize towels)*

FITS 8 X 10 FRAME | FOR FUTURE USE, A PRINTABLE PDF CAN BE PURCHASED AT **PDFCALLIGRAPHY.COM**   24

Only A Bridge

My desire for you is not to cry.
I don't believe in saying good bye.
Awake each morning instead and say
Hello to another God-given day.
For in it you will see me there;
Memories of me are everywhere.
And though I'm not within your view
A piece of me is a part of you.
So cherish each moment we happened to spend,
For where I left off you will begin.
'Tis only a bridge from you to me;
Some glorious day you too will see
That this precious life which
experiences death is really
only a fleeting breath compared
to the breadth of eternity.
For in an instant God set me free.
Grieve not for what you think
was lost, but rejoice in the
one who paid the cost.
For the Savior chose to
die that day:
His glorious sacrifice paved the way.
Christ built a bridge as only He could
With only three nails and two pieces of wood.

~Mary Kay Brewster

Safe In His Arms

I was just a little one when my Father took me home.
In fact, I wasn't even born; I was in my mother's womb.

And though my tiny features were not yet fully formed,
My parents still anticipated the day that I'd be born.

But now my Father took me to dwell with Him above.
My parents naturally question the wisdom of His love.

No heartache can compare with the death of one small being,
even though that little one had never yet been seen.

I, too, want to question why so soon I had to go.
But this one thing I'm certain, my Father loves me so.

He surely must have known what was best for Mom and Dad,
even though for now their hearts are very sad.

Don't worry my dear parents; to me there is no harm.
I'm dwelling up in heaven. I'm safe within His arms.

So try not to be sad now. For me you need not weep.
I'm looking for the day now for us to some day meet.

~Mary Kay Brewster

My Very Best Friend

He sits, he begs, he gives a paw;
my very best friend of sorts.
All too soon he left us
and now, he's missed, of course.

There's got to be a resting place
for a creature so Divine.
I'm glad I had a chance to say
this precious dog was mine.

So, until we meet again my friend,
I'll hold you in my heart.
Mere words cannot express sweet boy,
how hard it is to part.

Mary Kay Brewster

PDFCalligraphy.com

My Very Best Friend

She sits, she begs, she gives a paw;
my very best friend of sorts.
All too soon she left us
and now, she's missed, of course.

There's got to be a resting place
for a creature so Divine.
I'm glad I had a chance to say
this precious dog was mine.

So, until we meet again my friend,
I'll hold you in my heart.
Mere words cannot express sweet girl,
how hard it is to part.

Mary Kay Brewster

PDFCalligraphy.com

CATEGORY: **BEREAVEMENT**   TITLE: **MY VERY BEST FRIEND** (female dog)

FITS 8 X 10 FRAME | FOR FUTURE USE, A PRINTABLE PDF CAN BE PURCHASED AT **PDFCALLIGRAPHY.COM**   28

My Brother

Thank you for being my very best friend,
for patiently sharing life's ups and downs.
For giving your time to listen and care,
your understanding spirit is always there.

You are the sunshine of all my glad days
the rainbow that brightens all my sad days.
When life offers thorns you're the rose among them.
No wonder I deem you my very best friend

No words can express my love and affection
as I humbly offer my appreciation
You are as good as a friend can be—
You are God's special gift to me.

Mary Kay Brewster ©95
PDFCalligraphy.com

CATEGORY: **BROTHER**   TITLE: **BROTHER THANK YOU**

FITS 8 X 10 FRAME | FOR FUTURE USE, A PRINTABLE PDF CAN BE PURCHASED AT **PDFCALLIGRAPHY.COM**

My Brother

I wish there was a path that led
from your back door to mine.
And when we took the notion
we could visit any time.

For we need a time to share;
a time to reminisce.
Your caring ways and radiant smile
are qualities that I miss.

I'll always be there for your needs;
best friends we'll always be.
Thank God we have a kinship
that will last eternally

I admire your strength and courage
with the trials that you have faced;
Your surrender and acceptance
that God alone provides you grace.

And though there's miles between us,
there never is a day
That I don't think about you;
you're only a thought away.

M.R. Brewster © '96   PDFCalligraphy.com

CATEGORY: **BROTHER**   TITLE: **MY BROTHER**

FITS 8 X 10 FRAME | FOR FUTURE USE, A PRINTABLE PDF CAN BE PURCHASED AT **PDFCALLIGRAPHY.COM**

This Lock of Hair

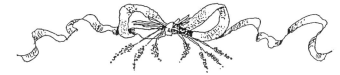

This lock of hair was carefully saved;
    a keepsake of younger years.
It reminds me of my childhood,
    a memory oh so dear.

My mother used to rock me close
    with my head tucked next to hers.
She pressed her cheek next to my hair
    and made me feel secure.

I remember my first haircut
    I sat up straight and still
I heard the scissors clip and snip
    as to the floor it fell.

My mother carefully picked it up.
    She has saved it through the years.
I'm reminded of her thoughtfulness.
    and how much she really cares.

PDFCalligraphy.com

−Mary Kay Brewster
©.96

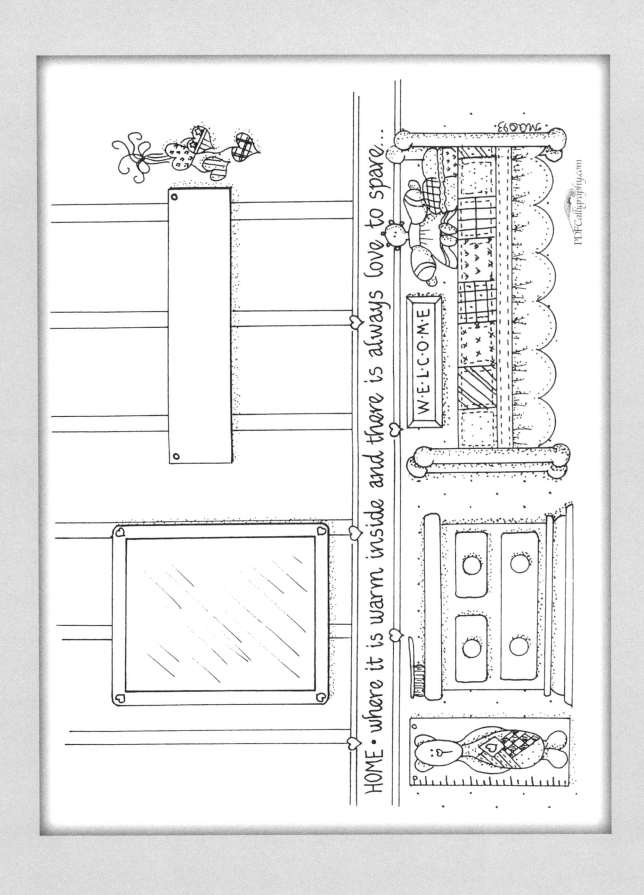

CATEGORY: **CHILDREN**   TITLE: **GIRL'S ROOM** (write child's name on plaque)

FITS 8 X 10 FRAME | FOR FUTURE USE, A PRINTABLE PDF CAN BE PURCHASED AT **PDFCALLIGRAPHY.COM**   32

CATEGORY: **CHILDREN**   TITLE: **BOY'S ROOM** (write child's name on plaque)

FITS 8 X 10 FRAME | FOR FUTURE USE, A PRINTABLE PDF CAN BE PURCHASED AT **PDFCALLIGRAPHY.COM**   33

Cherish the fingerprints
you find on your mirror...
you find they get higher
and soon disappear

PDFCalligraphy.com

CATEGORY: **CHILDREN**   TITLE: **CHERISH THE FINGERPRINTS**

FITS 8 X 10 FRAME | FOR FUTURE USE, A PRINTABLE PDF CAN BE PURCHASED AT **PDFCALLIGRAPHY.COM**

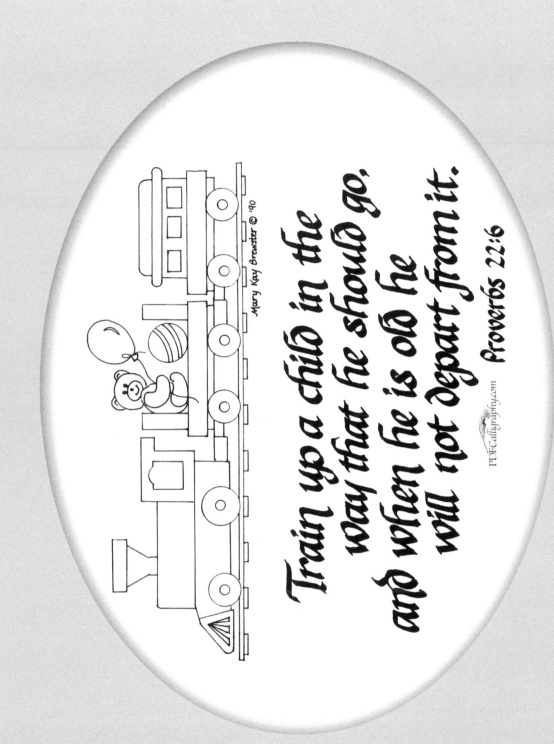

Train up a child in the way that he should go, and when he is old he will not depart from it. Proverbs 22:6

Mary Kay Brewster © '90

PDFCalligraphy.com

CATEGORY: **CHILDREN**   TITLE: **TRAIN UP A CHILD**

FITS 8 X 10 FRAME | FOR FUTURE USE, A PRINTABLE PDF CAN BE PURCHASED AT **PDFCALLIGRAPHY.COM**   35

Hand in Hand

I made my handprint next to yours
just so I can recall
That one day I was very young
and innocent and small.

And someday when I'm grown,
my hand I'll place on here.
I imagine I will be amazed
how much I've grown each year

I'll look back and remember
all the times you took my hand,
To lead me carefully through life,
to help me understand.

The lessons that I will have learned
by your hand strong and sure
Will prepare me for the path ahead
and forevermore endure.

Mary Kay Brewster ©95

PDFCalligraphy.com

CATEGORY: **CHILDREN**   TITLE: **HAND IN HAND - BOY** (personalize & add handprints)

FITS 8 X 10 FRAME | FOR FUTURE USE, A PRINTABLE PDF CAN BE PURCHASED AT **PDFCALLIGRAPHY.COM**

Hand in Hand

I made my handprint next to yours
    just so I can recall
That one day I was very young
    and innocent and small.

And someday when I'm grown,
    my hand I'll place on here.
I imagine I will be amazed
    how much I've grown each year

I'll look back and remember
    all the times you took my hand;
To lead me carefully through life,
    to help me understand.

The lessons that I will have learned
    by your hand strong and sure
Will prepare me for the path ahead
    and forevermore endure.

Mary Kay Brewster ©'95

PDFCalligraphy.com

CATEGORY: **CHILDREN**   TITLE: **HAND IN HAND - GIRL** (personalize & add hand prints)

FITS 8 X 10 FRAME | FOR FUTURE USE, A PRINTABLE PDF CAN BE PURCHASED AT **PDFCALLIGRAPHY.COM**   37

Sitting on Santa's Lap

He's no stranger in these parts;
the man with the red velvet hat.
And once again as tradition would have it,
I'm sitting on his lap.

I've made my list. I've checked it twice.
I'm ready with my requests.
And soon he'll ask "the question".
I hope I pass the test.

"I've been a pretty good kid this year.
What do you think of that?"
"Now what do you want for Christmas?" he asks,
as he gives my head a pat.

And though my list is a little long
he patiently sits and listens.
Sitting on Santa's lap is, for sure,
my favorite Christmas tradition.

~Mary Kay Brewster

PDFCalligraphy.com

Crayons Can Be Anything

I have a little crayon box that's shiny and new;
    eight crayons lined up neatly, in all my favorite hues.
My crayons are such fun to use. I spread them on the floor.
    The colors then remind me of when I go outdoors.

Red is the color of the perfect little rose.
    Black is for the bumblebee that landed on my nose.
Orange is the robin that is learning how to fly.
    Blue is for the open space created by the sky.

Purple's for the grapes I picked while standing on a chair.
    Brown is for the tree stump that looks so worn and bare.
Green is for the trees that grow, oh, so very high.
    Yellow's for the sunshine in the corner of the sky.

Red and yellow, orange and blue,
    black and brown, and green and purple, too;
colors that are everywhere if we just look around,
    colors in my crayon box, it's hard to put them down.

So if you have a crayon box and need something to do,
    just choose your favorite colors and draw a thing or two.
Crayons can be anything that you would have them be.
    So, open up your crayon box and all these things you'll see.

~Mary Kay Brewster   PDFCalligraphy.com

CATEGORY: **CHILDREN**   TITLE: **CRAYONS CAN BE ANYTHING**

FITS 8 X 10 FRAME | FOR FUTURE USE, A PRINTABLE PDF CAN BE PURCHASED AT **PDFCALLIGRAPHY.COM**   39

Cousins

Many good times we share
and the laughter we savor.
Though we're cousins by chance
it's your friendship I favor.

Is it no wonder
that you're special to me?
After all we descended
from the same family tree.

For cousins are bonded
with a special kind of kinship.
Over time we've developed
a rare kind of friendship.

~Mary Kay Brewster

PDFCalligraphy.com

CATEGORY: **COUSINS**   TITLE: **COUSINS**

FITS 8 X 10 FRAME | FOR FUTURE USE, A PRINTABLE PDF CAN BE PURCHASED AT **PDFCALLIGRAPHY.COM**   40

Daddy's Boy

Daddy, oh daddy, come wash the car,
empty the trash and mow the yard.
Hoe the garden and plant the seeds,
pay the bills and pull the weeds.
Where is the daddy whose work is undone?
He's out in the yard playing cowboys and guns.
Oh, I've grown as useless as an old basset hound.
(bang, bang, pow, pow, or so goes the sound).
Chores are waiting, the dog has a flea,
(giddyup horsy upon daddy's knee).
Oh, hoeing and planting I'll do another time.
For boys become men at the turn of a dime.
So lie still worrisome chores, don't give a care.
My boy wants to play now… there's no time to spare.

Mary Kay Brewster

PDFCalligraphy.com

CATEGORY: **DAD**   TITLE: **DADDY'S BOY** (can be hand colored)

FITS 8 X 10 FRAME | FOR FUTURE USE, A PRINTABLE PDF CAN BE PURCHASED AT **PDFCALLIGRAPHY.COM**

Daddy's Boys

Daddy, oh daddy, come wash the car,
empty the trash and mow the yard.
Hoe the garden and plant the seeds,
pay the bills and pull the weeds.
Where is the daddy whose work is undone?
He's out in the yard playing cowboys and guns.
Oh, I've grown as useless as an old basset hound.
(bang, bang, pow, pow, or so goes the sound).
Chores are waiting, the dog has a flea,
(giddyup horsy upon daddy's knee).
Oh, hoeing and planting I'll do another time.
For boys become men at the turn of a dime.
So lie still worrisome chores, don't give a care.
My boys want to play now… there's no time to spare.

Mary Kay Brewster

PDFCalligraphy.com

CATEGORY: **DAD**   TITLE: **DADDY'S BOYS** (can be hand colored)

Daddy's Girl

Daddy, oh daddy, come wash the car,
empty the trash and mow the yard.
Hoe the garden and plant the seeds,
pay the bills and pull the weeds.
Where is the daddy whose work is undone?
He's reading a book to his daughter for fun.
Oh, I've grown as useless as an old basset hound.
(Once upon a time... or so goes the sound).
Chores are waiting, the dog has a flea,
(read me a story upon daddy's knee).
Oh, hoeing and planting I'll do another time.
For girls become grown at the turn of a dime.
So lie still worrisome chores, don't give a care.
My girl wants to play now... there's no time to spare.

Mary Kay Brewster

PDFCalligraphy.com

CATEGORY: **DAD**   TITLE: **DADDY'S GIRL** (can be hand colored)

Daddy's Girls

Daddy, oh daddy, come wash the car,
empty the trash and mow the yard.
Hoe the garden and plant the seeds,
pay the bills and pull the weeds.
Where is the daddy whose work is undone?
He's reading a book to his daughters for fun.
Oh, I've grown as useless as an old basset hound.
(Once upon a time... or so goes the sound).
Chores are waiting, the dog has a flea,
(read me a story upon daddy's knee).
Oh, hoeing and planting I'll do another time.
For girls become grown at the turn of a dime.
So lie still worrisome chores, don't give a care.
My girls want to play now... there's no time to spare.

Mary Kay Brewster

PDFCalligraphy.com

CATEGORY: **DAD**   TITLE: **DADDY'S GIRLS** (can be hand colored)

Daddy's Little Girl

She's following at his heels
just begging to go along;
Washing the car together
and singing a silly song.
She's riding on his shoulders
laughing on his knee;
A pair where love is mutual
and very plain to see.
She's like him in so many ways,
from her toes up to her curls.
So cry your eyes out mommy~
she's Daddy's Little Girl.

~Mary Kay Brewster

PDFCalligraphy.com

CATEGORY: **DAD**   TITLE: **DADDY'S LITTLE GIRL** (can be hand colored)

FITS 8 X 10 FRAME | FOR FUTURE USE, A PRINTABLE PDF CAN BE PURCHASED AT **PDFCALLIGRAPHY.COM**

Dad

You've been a special blessing
  in my life, there is no doubt.
With consistent love and caring
  I've never been without.

To watch you go to work each day
  and never once complain,
You've been a true example, Dad,
  you've shown me how to gain.

To gain not only wealth and things;
  you've shown me greater treasure.
You taught me how to gain respect
  and love that can't be measured.

I won't forget the time you shared;
  you sacrificed for sure.
And when my life seemed broken
  you always knew the cure.

I'll always be your little girl;
  my love I cannot hide.
I'm glad to call you "Dad"
  I speak your name with pride.

Mary Kay Brewster ©'95

PDFCalligraphy.com

CATEGORY: **DAD**   TITLE: **DAD — FROM DAUGHTER**

FITS 8 X 10 FRAME | FOR FUTURE USE, A PRINTABLE PDF CAN BE PURCHASED AT **PDFCALLIGRAPHY.COM**   46

Dad

You've been a special blessing
   in my life, there is no doubt.
With consistent love and caring
   I've never been without.

To watch you go to work each day
   and never once complain,
You've been a true example, Dad,
   you've shown me how to gain.

To gain not only wealth and things;
   you've shown me greater treasure.
You taught me how to gain respect
   and love that can't be measured.

I won't forget the time you shared;
   you sacrificed for sure.
And when my life seemed broken
   you always knew the cure.

I'll always be your gracious son;
   my love I cannot hide.
I'm glad to call you "Dad"
   I speak your name with pride.

Mary Kay Brewster ©'95

PDFCalligraphy.com

CATEGORY: **DAD**   TITLE: **DAD — FROM SON**

FITS 8 X 10 FRAME | FOR FUTURE USE, A PRINTABLE PDF CAN BE PURCHASED AT **PDFCALLIGRAPHY.COM**

Dad

Thank you for being my very best friend,
for patiently sharing life's ups and downs.
For giving your time to listen and care,—
your understanding spirit is always there.

You are the sunshine of all my glad days
the rainbow that brightens all my sad days.
When life offers thorns you're the rose among them.
No wonder I deem you my very best friend

No words can express my love and affection
as I humbly offer my appreciation
You are as good as a friend can be—
You are God's special gift to me.

Mary Kay Brewster

PDFCalligraphy.com

CATEGORY: **DAD**   TITLE: **DAD THANK YOU**

FITS 8 X 10 FRAME | FOR FUTURE USE, A PRINTABLE PDF CAN BE PURCHASED AT **PDFCALLIGRAPHY.COM**   48

All the years that I've known you
since you brought me home that day.
You've been a wonderful father —
in every single way.

You've shown me how a dad should be
in all your ways and deeds.
You've taught me every thing I know
to prosper and succeed.

And when a friend I needed —,
you were always there.
To encourage and uplift me —
and show you really care.

DAD

CATEGORY: **DAD**   TITLE: **DAD ALL THE YEARS**

FITS 8 X 10 FRAME | FOR FUTURE USE, A PRINTABLE PDF CAN BE PURCHASED AT **PDFCALLIGRAPHY.COM**   49

Single Dad

♥♥♥♥♥♥♥♥♥♥♥♥♥♥♥

You dress me, feed me, play with me
and tuck me in at night.
And when I have a boo boo
you kiss and make it right.

You work so hard to pay the bills,
you never miss a day.
And still somehow you find the time
to take me out to play.

I sit and ponder and I think
of all the things you do.
But most of all I'm amazed
at how you do the job of two.

-Mary Kay Brewster

PDFCalligraphy.com

My Daddy's Heart

My daddy's heart is tender. My daddy's heart is kind.
And with his heartfelt wisdom he always makes me mind.
And I don't always heed his word. Sometimes I go astray.
But it's just like my daddy's heart to love me anyway.

My daddy's time is special. He knows it's not his own.
He spends his time to help me. He knows I'll soon be grown.
He teaches me to love the Lord through all his ways and deeds.
He takes the time to answer me and gives me all my needs.

My daddy's hands are gentle. My daddy's hands are strong.
He uses them to serve the Lord. He works the whole day long.
And when at night I go to bed he gives my back a rub.
And then he says a quiet prayer, and thanks the Lord above.

Just like my Heavenly Father, he's my guardian and my guide.
I know that I can count on him to be there by my side.

~Mary Kay Brewster

PDFCalligraphy.com

CATEGORY: **DAD**   TITLE: **MY DADDY'S HEART**

FITS 8 X 10 FRAME | FOR FUTURE USE, A PRINTABLE PDF CAN BE PURCHASED AT **PDFCALLIGRAPHY.COM**   51

A Father's Prayer

I come to you with humility
and a burdened heart today.
Please give me wisdom, courage and strength
as on my knees I pray.
Teach me Lord to follow You
and bestow on me Your power.
And help me to depend on You
with each passing hour.
Bless my home and family
and give me what I need
to be the leader of my home
in all my words and deeds.
May I not forget to thank you Lord
for the promises You keep.
A man of God I want to be
as my family I lead.

~Mary Kay Brewster

PDFCalligraphy.com

CATEGORY: **DAD**　　　TITLE: **A FATHER'S PRAYER**

FITS 8 X 10 FRAME | FOR FUTURE USE, A PRINTABLE PDF CAN BE PURCHASED AT **PDFCALLIGRAPHY.COM**

Like a Dad

You've been just like a dad to me—
in every single way.
Mere words cannot express my thanks
for all you do and say.

Your words of wisdom I cherish,
and memories will I treasure.
Your dad –like ways are dear to me;
your friendship can't be measured.

The special kinship that we have—
was destined from the start.
Even though I'm not your son
I love you with all my heart.

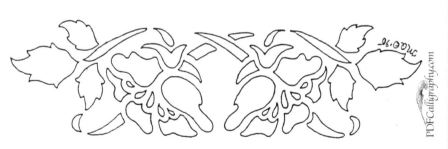

PDFcalligraphy.com

CATEGORY: **DAD**   TITLE: **LIKE A DAD**

Daughter

All the years that we've known you you've been so inclined
To be different and daring; to be one of a kind.
You've never been afraid to go it alone.
You have strength and courage and a mind of your own.

You demonstrate confidence no matter the test,
And we've never seen you give less than your best.
We're proud of the wisdom and lesson you've learned;
That respect from others can only be earned.

Your strong wit and humor are also a part
Of making us happy and touching our hearts.
Your caring and sharing and love combined
Work together, daughter, to make you one of a kind.

Mary Kay Brewster © 95

PDFCalligraphy.com

CATEGORY: **DAUGHTER**   TITLE: **DAUGHTER ALL THE YEARS**

FITS 8 X 10 FRAME | FOR FUTURE USE, A PRINTABLE PDF CAN BE PURCHASED AT **PDFCALLIGRAPHY.COM**   54

My daughter, my kin,
devoted and caring.
My daughter, my friend
in confidence sharing.

Sharing our ideas
our joys and sorrows
Sharing our dreams
and all our tomorrows.

My daughter, my friend,
loving and kind.
You're special to me.
I'm glad you're mine.

Mary Kay Brewster ©'95

PDFCalligraphy.com

CATEGORY: **DAUGHTER**   TITLE: **MY DAUGHTER MY KIN** (can be personalized)

A daughter
is a special treasure;
her mother's joy,
her father's pride.
To everyone she gives
such pleasures;
happiness beyond
all measure.

CATEGORY: **DAUGHTER**   TITLE: **A DAUGHTER IS**

FITS 8 X 10 FRAME | FOR FUTURE USE, A PRINTABLE PDF CAN BE PURCHASED AT **PDFCALLIGRAPHY.COM**

God blessed me twice
when He gave me you;
a daughter
and a best friend too.

Mary Kay Brewster ©93

PDFCalligraphy.com

CATEGORY: **DAUGHTER**   TITLE: **GOD BLESS ME** (daughter)

FITS 8 X 10 FRAME | FOR FUTURE USE, A PRINTABLE PDF CAN BE PURCHASED AT **PDFCALLIGRAPHY.COM**

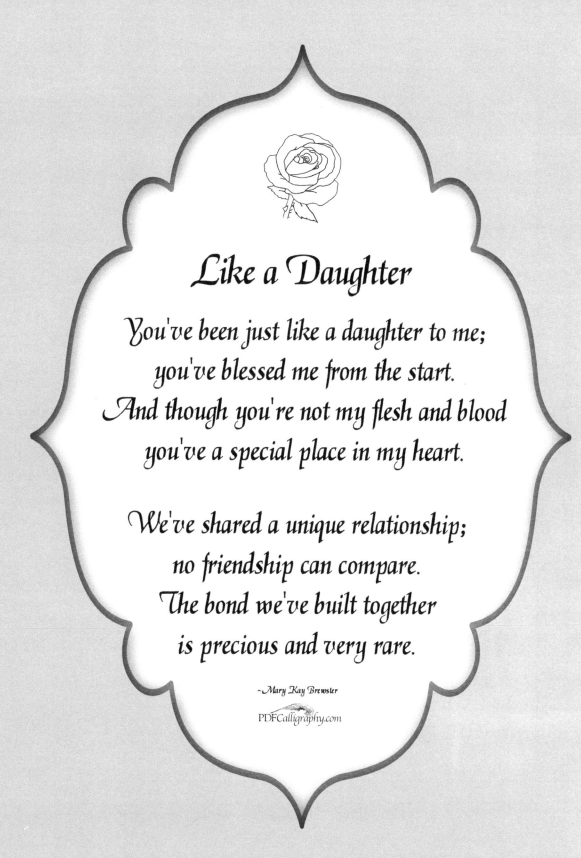

Like a Daughter

You've been just like a daughter to me;
you've blessed me from the start.
And though you're not my flesh and blood
you've a special place in my heart.

We've shared a unique relationship;
no friendship can compare.
The bond we've built together
is precious and very rare.

~Mary Kay Brewster

PDFCalligraphy.com

CATEGORY: **DAUGHTER**   TITLE: **LIKE A DAUGHTER**

FITS 8 X 10 FRAME | FOR FUTURE USE, A PRINTABLE PDF CAN BE PURCHASED AT **PDFCALLIGRAPHY.COM**

I knew when I met you
that you were the one,—
The sweet loving woman
who would marry my son.

And now that I've known you
there is no mistake,—
He instinctively chose you
to be his life's mate.

You are the daughter-in-law
for which I have longed,
And now to this family
you truly belong.—

Please always remember
as we learn to relate,—
You're loved like a daughter;
in you I have faith.

Mary Kay Brewster ©94 PDFCalligraphy.com

CATEGORY: DAUGHTER-IN-LAW TITLE: **I KNEW WHEN I MET YOU**

FITS 8 X 10 FRAME | FOR FUTURE USE, A PRINTABLE PDF CAN BE PURCHASED AT **PDFCALLIGRAPHY.COM**

Our Family Creed

A close and loving family
is a goal for which we strive;
To recognize each other's strengths
and bless each other's lives.

We understand that each of us
has a seed to sow.
We nurture one another
and help each other grow.

We stand up for each other
no matter come what may.
When we accomplish something good
we give each other praise.

We don't forget to thank the Lord
for all His blessings true.
We give Him praise and honor
for He's a member too.

PDFCalligraphy.com   –Mary Kay Brewster
© '96

CATEGORY: **FAMILY**   TITLE: **OUR FAMILY CREED**

FITS 8 X 10 FRAME | FOR FUTURE USE, A PRINTABLE PDF CAN BE PURCHASED AT **PDFCALLIGRAPHY.COM**

Our house is just a little place...

But God knows where we live

Mary Kay Brewster ©94
PDFCalligraphy.com

Thinking of You

I wish there was a path that led
from your back door to mine.
And when we took the notion
we could visit any time.

No doubt there'd be a well-worn trail
from my back door to yours
I'd visit you quite often;
we'd chat and laugh for hours.

Regretfully we're kept apart
with many miles between.
That only makes our friendship
grow stronger than it seems.

For with long miles between us,
there never is a day
That I don't think about you;
you're one short thought away.

WELCOME

MQ©95

CATEGORY: **FRIENDSHIP**   TITLE: **THINKING OF YOU**

FITS 8 X 10 FRAME | FOR FUTURE USE, A PRINTABLE PDF CAN BE PURCHASED AT **PDFCALLIGRAPHY.COM**   62

My Best Friend

Thank you for being my very best friend,
for patiently sharing life's ups and downs.
For giving your time to listen and care,
your understanding spirit is always there.

You are the sunshine of all my glad days
the rainbow that brightens all my sad days.
When life offers thorns you're the rose among them.
No wonder I deem you my very best friend

No words can express my love and affection
as I humbly offer my appreciation
You are as good as a friend can be—
You are God's special gift to me.

Mary Kay Brewster ©95
PDFCalligraphy.com

CATEGORY: **FRIENDSHIP**   TITLE: **MY BEST FRIEND**

FITS 8 X 10 FRAME | FOR FUTURE USE, A PRINTABLE PDF CAN BE PURCHASED AT **PDFCALLIGRAPHY.COM**   63

Three things
that make

Life worth living:
GOD, friends, and
Chocolate-Chip
Cookies!

CATEGORY: **FRIENDSHIP**   TITLE: **THREE THINGS**

FITS 8 X 10 FRAME | FOR FUTURE USE, A PRINTABLE PDF CAN BE PURCHASED AT **PDFCALLIGRAPHY.COM**   64

Graduate

We watched you grow over the years
and nurtured you from the start.
We tried to teach you right from wrong
and loved you with all our hearts.

We saw you through the tough times;
we were with you through the good.
What ever trials the day would bring
you always knew where we stood.

But now our job is completed
and your childhood seems farther away.
You now have reached a turning point
as you tackle this new day.

So as you decide your future
and plan the path you'll take,
Remember we're right behind you
supporting you all the way.

PDFCalligraphy.com

~ MK Brewster © '96

CATEGORY: **GRADUATE**   TITLE: **GRADUATE WE WATCHED**

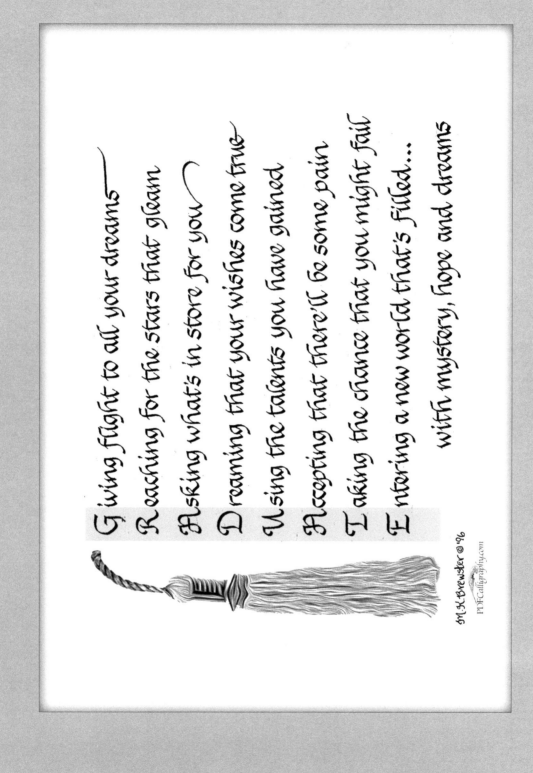

Giving flight to all your dreams
Reaching for the stars that gleam
Asking what's in store for you
Dreaming that your wishes come true
Using the talents you have gained
Accepting that there'll be some pain
Taking the chance that you might fail
Entering a new world that's filled...
with mystery, hope and dreams

M.K.Brewster @ '96
PDFCalligraphy.com

CATEGORY: **GRADUATE**   TITLE: **GRADUATE — GIVING FLIGHT**

FITS 8 X 10 FRAME | FOR FUTURE USE, A PRINTABLE PDF CAN BE PURCHASED AT **PDFCALLIGRAPHY.COM**

May you feel pride in all that you are and find joy in all you have yet to be.

PDFCalligraphy.com

CATEGORY: **GRADUATE**   TITLE: **MAY YOU FEEL** (ribbon can be personalized)

FITS 8 X 10 FRAME | FOR FUTURE USE, A PRINTABLE PDF CAN BE PURCHASED AT **PDFCALLIGRAPHY.COM**

Grandma Cares

I know my grandma cares for me
and this is how I know;
She gently sets me on her lap
and rocks me to and fro.
She tells me stories of days gone by
and sings me little songs.
And though the hours pass us by
it doesn't seem that long.
She makes me feel so all grown up.
I make her feel real young.
Sometimes I have to wonder if
by her the moon was hung.

~Mary Kay Brewster

PDFCalligraphy.com

CATEGORY: **GRANDMA**   TITLE: **GRANDMA CARES**

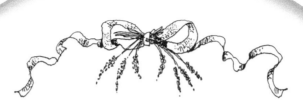

Grandma

I love my Grandma very much
and I know that she loves me.
She sparkles when she sees me
and her eyes light up with glee.

She fills my days with happy times
and the special things she shares,
Shows me I'm important —
shows me how she cares.

She's someone very loving,
and I'm glad that I'm a part
Of an understanding Grandma
with a young and happy heart.

Mary Kay Brewster   *PDFCalligraphy.com*

CATEGORY: **GRANDMA**   TITLE: **GRANDMA I LOVE**

If I
had known
grandchildren
were this much
fun, I would
have had them
first.

MQ© 94

PDFCalligraphy.com

CATEGORY: **GRANDMA**   TITLE: **IF I HAD KNOWN** (can be hand colored)

FITS 8 X 10 FRAME | FOR FUTURE USE, A PRINTABLE PDF CAN BE PURCHASED AT **PDFCALLIGRAPHY.COM**   70

Grandma

grandmas are a special breed
    they share so very much
they seem to spread old-fashioned
    charm to everything they touch

grandmas take a certain pride
    in all the things they know
for through their years of wisdom
    we hear and learn and grow

grandmas can be special friends
    they show a loving care
they give us much encouragement
    for they have time to spare

PDFCalligraphy.com   ~ M.K. BREWSTER © '90

CATEGORY: **GRANDMA**   TITLE: **GRANDMAS ARE A SPECIAL BREED**

Grandparents

Grandparents are a special pair,
  they share so very much___.
They seem to spread old-fashioned
  charm to everything they touch.

Grandparents take a certain pride
  in all the things they know.
For through their years of wisdom
  we see and learn and grow.

Grandparents can be special friends,
  they show us love and care.
They give us much encouragement,
  their time they freely share.

PDFCalligraphy.com

— SK Brewster

I'm glad I have a granddaughter
with whom I can relate.
    We have so much in common
it really is a sight.

    When we walk together
her steps are in time with mine.
    And when we get real busy
we have no sense of time.

    I talk about her future.
She asks about my past.
    And with our conversations
we make memories that last.

    I think of her as all grown up
She thinks that I'm still young.
    Make no mistake about it
by her the moon was hung.

Mary Kay Brewster PDFCalligraphy.com

CATEGORY: **GRANDPARENTS**   TITLE: **I'M GLAD I HAVE A GRANDDAUGHTER**

FITS 8 X 10 FRAME | FOR FUTURE USE, A PRINTABLE PDF CAN BE PURCHASED AT **PDFCALLIGRAPHY.COM**

I'm glad I have a grandson
with whom I can relate.
We have so much in common
it really is a sight.

When we walk together
his steps are in time with mine.
And when we get real busy
we have no sense of time.

I talk about his future,
he asks about my past.
And with our conversations
we make memories that last.

I think of him as all grown up,
he thinks that I'm still young.
Make no mistake about it
by him the moon was hung.

Mary Kay Brewster PDFCalligraphy.com

CUT ALONG DOTTED LINE

The road to a friend's house is never long

We're glad to have you as our guest, and
hope you have a good night's rest.
Tomorrow you again may roam.
But while you're here just
feel at home.

PDFCalligraphy.com

CATEGORY: **HOME**   TITLE: **GUEST ROOM PLAQUE** (can be personalized)

FITS 8 X 10 FRAME | FOR FUTURE USE, A PRINTABLE PDF CAN BE PURCHASED AT **PDFCALLIGRAPHY.COM**   **75**

House Blessing

As you settle here
in your new nest
We as your friends
wish you the best
Remember as you
make this start
Home is where you
hang your heart
Within these blessed
walls so new
May happiness
abound for you

-Mary Kay Brewster

PDFCalligraphy.com

CATEGORY: **HOME**   TITLE: **HOUSE BLESSING**

FITS 8 X 10 FRAME | FOR FUTURE USE, A PRINTABLE PDF CAN BE PURCHASED AT **PDFCALLIGRAPHY.COM**

HOUSE RULES

If you open it.............close it
If you turn it on......turn it off
If you drop it.........pick it up
If you wear it.........hang it up
If you dirty it..........wash it
If you sleep in it......make it up
If you get it out.........put it up
If it rings.............answer it
If it hurts...........comfort it
If it cries..............love it

WELCOME

MQ©93

PDFCalligraphy.com

CATEGORY: **HOME**   TITLE: **HOUSE RULES** (can be hand colored and personalized)

FITS 8 X 10 FRAME | FOR FUTURE USE, A PRINTABLE PDF CAN BE PURCHASED AT **PDFCALLIGRAPHY.COM**   77

CATEGORY: **HOME**   TITLE: **HOUSE WELCOME — 1 CHILD** (personalize & color)

FITS 8 X 10 FRAME | FOR FUTURE USE, A PRINTABLE PDF CAN BE PURCHASED AT **PDFCALLIGRAPHY.COM**

CATEGORY: **HOME**   TITLE: **HOUSE WELCOME — 2 CHILDREN** (personalize & color)

CUT ALONG DOTTED LINE

CATEGORY: **HOME**   TITLE: **HOUSE WELCOME — 3 CHILDREN** (personalize & color)

FITS 8 X 10 FRAME | FOR FUTURE USE, A PRINTABLE PDF CAN BE PURCHASED AT **PDFCALLIGRAPHY.COM**   80

CATEGORY: **HOME**   TITLE: **HOUSE WELCOME — 4 CHILDREN** (personalize & color)

FITS 8 X 10 FRAME | FOR FUTURE USE, A PRINTABLE PDF CAN BE PURCHASED AT **PDFCALLIGRAPHY.COM**   81

CATEGORY: **HOME**   TITLE: **HOUSE WELCOME — 5 CHILDREN** (personalize & color)

Weights & Measures

3 teaspoons ... 1 tablespoon

4 tablespoons ... ¼ cup

5⅓ tablespoons ... ⅓ cup

8 tablespoons ... ½ cup

1 cup ... 8 fluid ounces

2 cups ... 1 pint

4 cups ... 1 quart

4 quarts ... 1 gallon

1 liter ... 1.06 quarts

CATEGORY: **HOME**   TITLE: **WEIGHTS AND MEASURES**

My Husband My Friend

I knew when I met you that I found a prize,
The moment I saw you and looked in your eyes.
And now that I'm with you there is no mistake,
I'm glad that you chose me to be your life's mate.

You've a strong arm to lean on, a heart that is true,
A shoulder to cry on when I'm feeling blue.
An ear to listen when I need a friend,
A firm chest to rest on at busy days end.

All these qualities you possess and more.
Is it no wonder it's you I adore...
My heart's overflowing with love for you.
You are my husband and best friend too.

PDFCalligraphy.com

CATEGORY: HUSBAND   TITLE: **MY HUSBAND MY FRIEND**

FITS 8 X 10 FRAME | FOR FUTURE USE, A PRINTABLE PDF CAN BE PURCHASED AT **PDFCALLIGRAPHY.COM**   84

My Wife My Friend

I was sure when I met you that you were my choice;
the moment I saw you and heard your sweet voice.
Your sweet loving spirit, your kind tender ways
make our years together seem only like days.

I'm blessed with a woman who's gentle yet strong.
I'm grateful to say it's with you I belong.
You've stood beside me through good times and bad.
You've been behind the successes I've had.

Your talents are numerous; your qualities true.
Is it no wonder that I love you......
No doubt each day on you I depend
You're not only my wife; you're also my friend.

PDFCalligraphy.com

—Mary Kay Brewster ©'05

CATEGORY: **WIFE**   TITLE: **MY WIFE MY FRIEND**

Faithful and Fruitful

Faithful and Fruitful I want to be,—
Just like my Father has been to me.—
He's faithful in all of His comings and goings;
Fruitful blessings from His hands are flowing.

Oh let me be faithful in all of my deeds
That I may be willing to plant fruitful seeds.
Seeds of kindness, compassion and love,—
Seeds that yield blessing and fruit from above.

God is so fruitful in all that He owns.—
He's faithful to give me a place by his throne.
Oh faithful and fruitful I want to be,—
Just like my Father has been to me.—

Mary Kay Brewster ©94

— MK Brewster

PDFCalligraphy.com

CATEGORY: **INSPIRATION**   TITLE: **FAITHFUL AND FRUITFUL**

A Servant's Heart

There is rarely one more special
than the person who has a goal
To serve the Lord and others
in a self forgetful role.

For talents are from Him alone;
your time is not your own.
God gives these gifts so graciously
to lay them at His throne.

If you give, it shall be given you
good measure and pressed down,
Shaken together and running over;
rich blessings will abound.

For when you give a part of yourself
and have a servant's heart
You inspire everyone around you
and you're reminded where
it starts... with you.

~Mary Kay Brewster
© '96

PDFCalligraphy.com

CATEGORY: **INSPIRATION/ SCRIPTURE**   TITLE: **A SERVANT'S HEART**

FITS 8 X 10 FRAME | FOR FUTURE USE, A PRINTABLE PDF CAN BE PURCHASED AT **PDFCALLIGRAPHY.COM**

GOD
Mary Kay Brewster © '88

GRANT ME
the SERENity to
accept the things
i cannot change
the couRage to change
those things i can
and the wisdom
to know the
diffeRence

PDFCalligraphy.com

CATEGORY: **INSPIRATION/ SCRIPTURE**   TITLE: **GOD GRANT ME**

FITS 8 X 10 FRAME | FOR FUTURE USE, A PRINTABLE PDF CAN BE PURCHASED AT **PDFCALLIGRAPHY.COM**   88

Serenity Prayer

God grant me the Serenity
to accept the things
I cannot change – Courage
to change the things
I can and the Wisdom
to know the difference.

Living One Day At A Time;
Accepting hardships as
the pathway to Peace;
Taking as He did, this
World as it is, Not as
I would have it.

Trusting that He will make
all things right if I surrender
to His will; That I may be
reasonably happy in this life
and Supremely Happy with
Him, Forever in the Next.

Reinhold Neibuhr – 1926

PDFCalligraphy.com

CATEGORY: **INSPIRATION/ SCRIPTURE**   TITLE: **SERENITY PRAYER (FULL)**

FITS 8 X 10 FRAME | FOR FUTURE USE, A PRINTABLE PDF CAN BE PURCHASED AT **PDFCALLIGRAPHY.COM**

CATEGORY: **INSPIRATION/ SCRIPTURE**   TITLE: **LET GO AND LET GOD**

I put all my eggs
in one basket...
and gave the basket
to God...

CATEGORY: **INSPIRATION/ SCRIPTURE**   TITLE: **I PUT ALL MY EGGS**

FITS 8 X 10 FRAME | FOR FUTURE USE, A PRINTABLE PDF CAN BE PURCHASED AT **PDFCALLIGRAPHY.COM**

Bless the Lord, O my soul,
and all that is within me
bless his holy name.

Bless the Lord, O my soul,
and forget not his benefits:

Who forgiveth all thine
iniquities; who healeth
all thy diseases;

Who redeemeth thy life
from destruction; who
crowneth thee with loving
kindness and tender mercies;

Who satisfieth thy mouth
with good things; so that
thy youth is renewed like
the eagles.

M.R.Brewster © 97

Psalm 103:1-5

PDFCalligraphy.com

CATEGORY: **INSPIRATION/ SCRIPTURE**   TITLE: **BLESS THE LORD**

FITS 8 X 10 FRAME | FOR FUTURE USE, A PRINTABLE PDF CAN BE PURCHASED AT **PDFCALLIGRAPHY.COM**

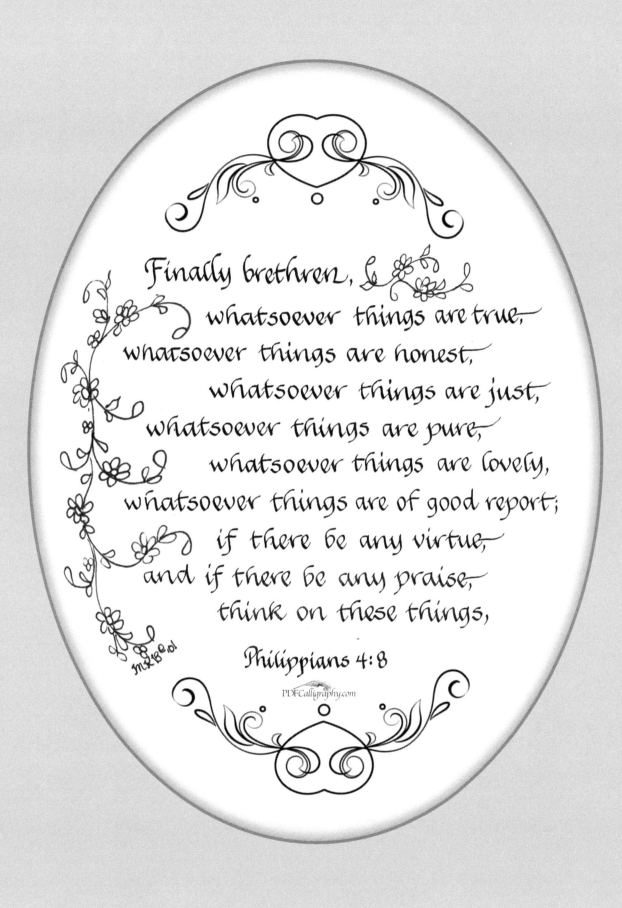

Finally brethren,
whatsoever things are true,
whatsoever things are honest,
whatsoever things are just,
whatsoever things are pure,
whatsoever things are lovely,
whatsoever things are of good report;
if there be any virtue,
and if there be any praise,
think on these things.

Philippians 4:8

PDFCalligraphy.com

CATEGORY: **INSPIRATION/ SCRIPTURE**   TITLE: **FINALLY BRETHREN**

But they that wait upon the Lord shall renew their strength they shall mount up with wings as eagles; they shall run and not be weary; they shall walk and not faint.

Isaiah 40:31

PDFCalligraphy.com

CATEGORY: **INSPIRATION/ SCRIPTURE**   TITLE: **BUT THEY THAT WAIT**

FITS 8 X 10 FRAME | FOR FUTURE USE, A PRINTABLE PDF CAN BE PURCHASED AT **PDFCALLIGRAPHY.COM**   94

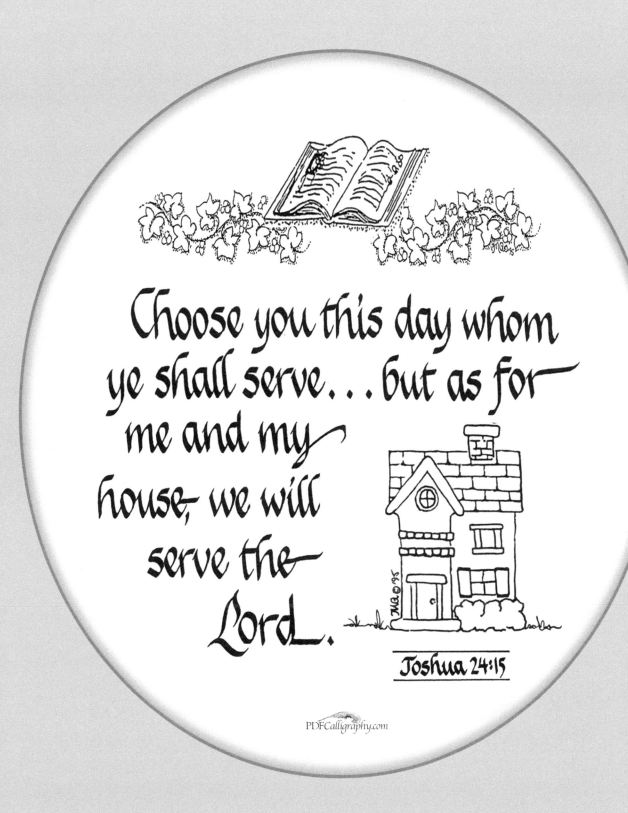

Choose you this day whom ye shall serve.... but as for me and my house, we will serve the Lord.

Joshua 24:15

PDFCalligraphy.com

CATEGORY: **INSPIRATION/ SCRIPTURE**   TITLE: **CHOOSE YOU THIS DAY**

FITS 8 X 10 FRAME | FOR FUTURE USE, A PRINTABLE PDF CAN BE PURCHASED AT **PDFCALLIGRAPHY.COM**

As the deer pants
for streams of water,
so my soul pants for
you, O God.

Psalm 42:1

PDFCalligraphy.com

CATEGORY: **INSPIRATION/ SCRIPTURE**   TITLE: **AS THE DEER**

FITS 8 X 10 FRAME | FOR FUTURE USE, A PRINTABLE PDF CAN BE PURCHASED AT **PDFCALLIGRAPHY.COM**

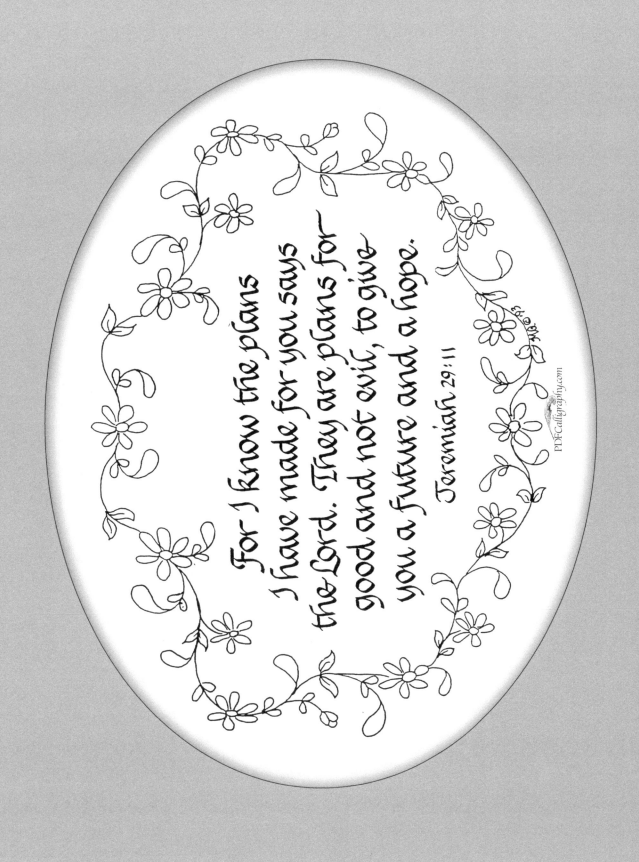

For I know the plans I have made for you says the Lord. They are plans for good and not evil, to give you a future and a hope.

Jeremiah 29:11

PDFCalligraphy.com

CATEGORY: **INSPIRATION/ SCRIPTURE**   TITLE: **FOR I KNOW THE PLANS**

FITS 8 X 10 FRAME | FOR FUTURE USE, A PRINTABLE PDF CAN BE PURCHASED AT **PDFCALLIGRAPHY.COM**   97

For God so loved the world,
that he gave his only begotten son,
that whosoever believeth in him
should not perish, but have
everlasting life.
John 3:16

PDFCalligraphy.com

CATEGORY: **INSPIRATION/ SCRIPTURE**   TITLE: **FOR GOD SO LOVED**

Mom

Thank you for being my very best friend,
for patiently sharing life's ups and downs.
For giving your time to listen and care,
your understanding spirit is always there.

You are the sunshine of all my glad days
the rainbow that brightens all my sad days.
When life offers thorns you're the rose among them.
No wonder I deem you my very best friend

No words can express my love and affection
as I humbly offer my appreciation
You are as good as a friend can be—
You are God's special gift to me.

PDFCalligraphy.com

CATEGORY: **MOM**   TITLE: **MOM THANK YOU**

FITS 8 X 10 FRAME | FOR FUTURE USE, A PRINTABLE PDF CAN BE PURCHASED AT **PDFCALLIGRAPHY.COM**

God blessed me twice
when he gave me you;
a mother
and a best friend too.

CATEGORY: **MOM**   TITLE: **GOD BLESSED ME - MOTHER**

FITS 8 X 10 FRAME | FOR FUTURE USE, A PRINTABLE PDF CAN BE PURCHASED AT **PDFCALLIGRAPHY.COM**   100

A mother holds her children's hands for a short while: their hearts forever.

CATEGORY: **MOM**   TITLE: **A MOTHER HOLDS** (can be personalized)

FITS 8 X 10 FRAME | FOR FUTURE USE, A PRINTABLE PDF CAN BE PURCHASED AT **PDFCALLIGRAPHY.COM**   101

My Other Mother

I'm glad I have a stepmom
that cares for me like you.
You came into my life one day
and gave me something new.

A new home and a new chance
to make the family whole.
What a challenge you have faced
to do my mother's role.

I know it's not that easy
to feel like second place.
But you have gained my confidence
as you this challenge face.

You sacrificed the life you knew
to give me a new start.
I can't express the trust and love
that's grown within my heart.

It's funny how that circumstances
as unusual as they seemed
Brought us both together
as a mother-daughter team.

Maya Kay Brewster © '95

PDFCalligraphy.com

Mom

You took on the job of Mother
Without even having a clue
Just how important your job would be
To see the family through

You saw me through the tough times
You were with me in the good
No matter what the day would bring
I always knew where you stood

You gave me rules and standards
And taught me right from wrong
You provided a sense of security
You made me glad to belong

I'm glad to belong to a family
With which you are a part
You are a Mom I'm proud of
And hold very dear to my

heart

PDFCalligraphy.com

CATEGORY: **MOM**   TITLE: **MOM YOU TOOK ON (STEP MOM)**

FITS 8 X 10 FRAME | FOR FUTURE USE, A PRINTABLE PDF CAN BE PURCHASED AT **PDFCALLIGRAPHY.COM**   103

Like a Mom

You've been just like a mom to me —
in every single way.
Mere words cannot express my thanks
for all you do and say.

Your words of wisdom I cherish —
and memories will I treasure.
Your mom-like ways are dear to me;
your friendship can't be measured.

The special kinship that we have —
was destined from the start.
Even though I'm not your daughter —
I love you with all my heart.

PDFCalligraphy.com

CATEGORY: **MOM**   TITLE: **LIKE A MOM**

Your Job is Done

Did you ever really realize—
    the job that was in store,
As you helped your daughter grow
    midst pigtails, frills and more.

Well, now it's time for you to know
    that I'm the grateful one.
You've raised a lovely daughter
    and now your job is done.

It's my turn to care for her.
    I'll marry her with pride.
I promise to protect her,
    to be there by her side.

I'll honor, love and cherish her
    as we this union start.
My attention and devotion
    I'll give with all my heart.

Remember now dear in-laws
    even though your job is done,
You haven't lost a daughter,
    you've only gained a son_____.

PDFCalligraphy.com   —Mary Kay Brewster
© 96

CATEGORY: **MOTHER-IN-LAW**   TITLE: **YOUR JOB IS DONE (FROM SON-IN-LAW)**

CUT ALONG DOTTED LINE

A Fireman's Prayer

Lord, You know our job is difficult;
we can't prevent the fires.
We can only salvage what is left.
That is all that's in our power.
So as we work around the clock,
help us stand the test.
Give us strength and endurance
and help us do our best.
Each time the alarm is sounded
give us courage to be brave.
May we count our efforts all worth while
with every life we save.
Fill us with compassion
as we examine the remains.
For no matter who experiences fire
we can't help but feel their pain.

Mary Kay Brewster *PDFCalligraphy.com*

CATEGORY: **OCCUPATION**   TITLE: **A FIREMAN'S PRAYER**

FITS 8 X 10 FRAME | FOR FUTURE USE, A PRINTABLE PDF CAN BE PURCHASED AT **PDFCALLIGRAPHY.COM**

Babysitter

You are the one I trust
to watch my child play;
to teach her right from wrong
whenever I'm away.

I leave her in your hands
to care for as I do.
I'm glad I found a babysitter
as caring as you.

PDFCalligraphy.com

CATEGORY: **OCCUPATION**   TITLE: **BABYSITTER (HER)**

FITS 8 X 10 FRAME | FOR FUTURE USE, A PRINTABLE PDF CAN BE PURCHASED AT **PDFCALLIGRAPHY.COM**   107

Babysitter

You are the one I trust
to watch my child play;
to teach him right from wrong
whenever I'm away.

I leave him in your hands
to care for as I do.
I'm glad I found a babysitter
as caring as you__.

PDFCalligraphy.com

CATEGORY: **OCCUPATION**   TITLE: **BABYSITTER (HIM)**

CUT ALONG DOTTED LINE

Babysitter

You are the one I trust
to watch my children play;
to teach them right from wrong
whenever I'm away.

I leave them in your hands
to care for as I do.
I'm glad I found a babysitter
as caring as you___.

PDFCalligraphy.com

CATEGORY: **OCCUPATION**   TITLE: **BABYSITTER (THEM) can be personalized**

How special you are;
how priceless you've grown.
You watch over children
as if they're your own.

Worlds Best

Baby Sitter

PDFCalligraphy.com

CATEGORY: **OCCUPATION**   TITLE: **HOW SPECIAL - BABYSITTER** (can be personalized)

FITS 8 X 10 FRAME | FOR FUTURE USE, A PRINTABLE PDF CAN BE PURCHASED AT **PDFCALLIGRAPHY.COM**   110

Beanie Baby Madness

There lie my little Beanie Babies lined up in several rows.
How this madness started no one really knows.
One by one I bought them, as cute as they could be;
Then Beanie Baby madness came completely over me.
Those furry little creatures, how sweetly they adorn;
Each one named appropriately with a date when they were born.
I'd call ahead and find out when they'd come in at the store.
The day of their arrival I'd camp out at the door.
And when the doors were opened the madness would begin.
I pushed my way between the crowd with shopping bag in hand.
I searched and grabbed and stuffed my bag 'til no more could go in it.
Would you believe those Beanies were gone in a measly five minutes?
My purse is drained, my feet are tired, I've shopped until I'm beat.
But I'll not stop this madness 'til my collection is complete.

~Mary Kay Brewster ~©'98

PDFCalligraphy.com

CATEGORY: **OCCUPATION**   TITLE: **COLLECTION (BEANIE BABY MADNESS)**

CATEGORY: **OCCUPATION**   TITLE: **NURSING IS A WORK**

How special you are;
how priceless you've grown.
You teach our children
as if they're your own.

World's Best Teacher

CATEGORY: **OCCUPATION**   TITLE: **TEACHER - HOW SPECIAL (can be personalized)**

FITS 8 X 10 FRAME | FOR FUTURE USE, A PRINTABLE PDF CAN BE PURCHASED AT **PDFCALLIGRAPHY.COM**   **113**

A teacher affects eternity;
he can never tell where—
his influence stops. —Henry Adams

PDFCalligraphy.com

CATEGORY: **OCCUPATION**   TITLE: **TEACHER - A TEACHERS AFFECTS**

CATEGORY: **OCCUPATION**   TITLE: **TEACHER - THE JOYS OF TEACHNG**

FITS 8 X 10 FRAME | FOR FUTURE USE, A PRINTABLE PDF CAN BE PURCHASED AT **PDFCALLIGRAPHY.COM**   115

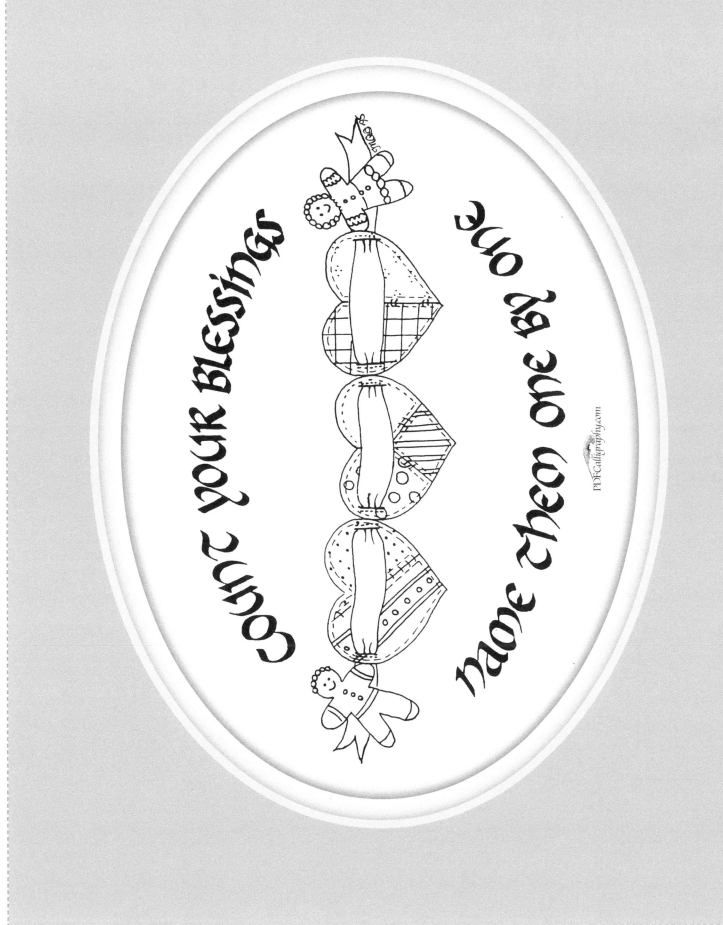

Count your blessings name them one by one

PDFCalligraphy.com

CATEGORY: **PARENTS**   TITLE: **COUNT YOUR BLESSINGS 3** (can be personalized)

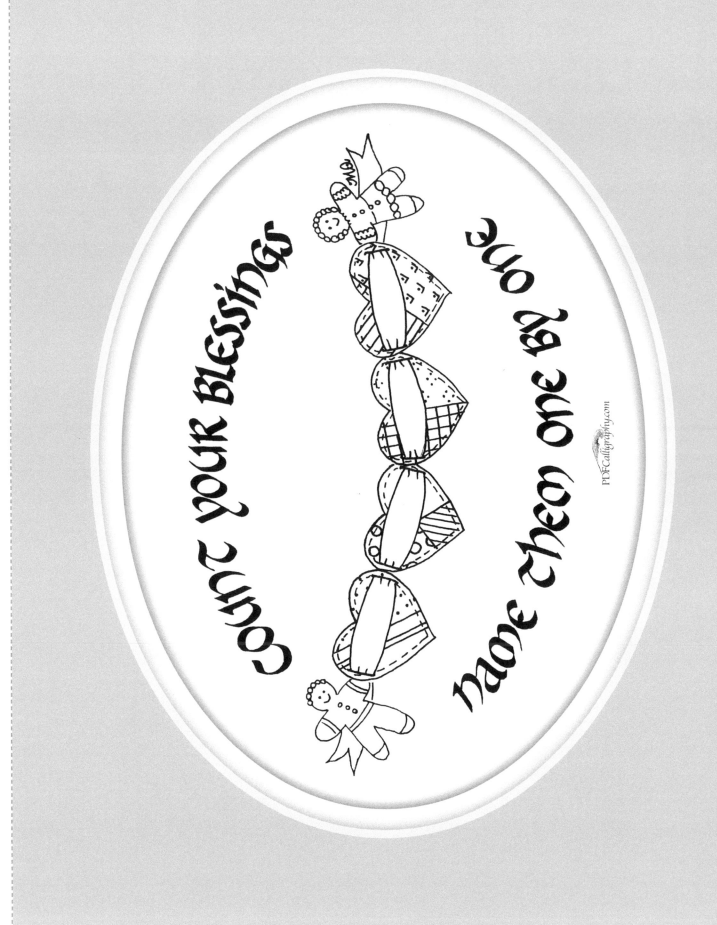

count your blessings

have them one by one

PDFcalligraphy.com

Parents hold their children's hands for a short while: their hearts forever.

CATEGORY: **PARENTS**　　　TITLE: **PARENTS HOLD 3** (can be personalized)

FITS 8 X 10 FRAME　|　FOR FUTURE USE, A PRINTABLE PDF CAN BE PURCHASED AT **PDFCALLIGRAPHY.COM**　118

Parents hold their children's hands for a short while: their hearts forever.

CATEGORY: **PARENTS**   TITLE: **PARENTS HOLD 4** (can be personalized)

FITS 8 X 10 FRAME | FOR FUTURE USE, A PRINTABLE PDF CAN BE PURCHASED AT **PDFCALLIGRAPHY.COM**   **119**

Like Parents

You've been just like parents to me;
you've blessed me from the start.
And though you're not my flesh and blood
you've a special place in my heart.

We've shared a unique relationship;
no friendship can compare.
The bond we've built together
is precious and very rare.

~Mary Kay Brewster

PDFCalligraphy.com

CATEGORY: **PARENTS**   TITLE: **LIKE PARENTS**

FITS 8 X 10 FRAME | FOR FUTURE USE, A PRINTABLE PDF CAN BE PURCHASED AT **PDFCALLIGRAPHY.COM**

Retirement is not the end of the road,

It is taking a new direction.

PDFcalligraphy.com

CATEGORY: **RETIREMENT**   TITLE: **RETIREMENT IS** (can be hand colored)

FITS 8 X 10 FRAME | FOR FUTURE USE, A PRINTABLE PDF CAN BE PURCHASED AT **PDFCALLIGRAPHY.COM**

God blessed me twice
when he gave me you;
a sister
and a best friend too.

PDFCalligraphy.com

To My Sister

Thank you for being my very best friend;
for patiently sharing life's ups and downs.
For giving your time to listen and care,—
your understanding spirit is always there.

You are the sunshine of all my glad days
the rainbow that brightens all my sad days.
When life offers thorns you're the rose among them.
No wonder I deem you my very best friend

No words can express my love and affection
as I humbly offer my appreciation
You are as good as a friend can be—
You are God's special gift to me.

PDFCalligraphy.com

CATEGORY: **SISTER**   TITLE: **TO MY SISTER**

FITS 8 X 10 FRAME | FOR FUTURE USE, A PRINTABLE PDF CAN BE PURCHASED AT **PDFCALLIGRAPHY.COM**   123

Chance made us sisters

H·E·A·R·T·S

made us friends.

CATEGORY: **SISTER**   TITLE: **CHANCE MADE US SISTERS**

My Sister

I wish there was a path that led
  from your back door to mine.
And when we took the notion
  we could visit any time.

For we need a time to share;
  a time to reminisce.
Your caring ways and radiant smile
  are qualities that I miss.

I'll always be there for your needs;
  best friends we'll always be.
Thank God we have a kinship
  that will last eternally

I admire your strength and courage
  with the trials that you have faced;
Your surrender and acceptance
  that God alone provides you grace.

And though there's miles between us,
  there never is a day
That I don't think about you;
  you're only a thought away.

M.K. Brewster © '96

PDFCalligraphy.com

CATEGORY: **SISTER**   TITLE: **MY SISTER (FAR AWAY)**

Three things that
make life worth living:

GOD, Sisters, and
Chocolate-Chip Cookies!

PDFCalligraphy.com

CATEGORY: **SISTER**   TITLE: **THREE THINGS (SISTER)**

FITS 8 X 10 FRAME | FOR FUTURE USE, A PRINTABLE PDF CAN BE PURCHASED AT **PDFCALLIGRAPHY.COM**

My Sister, my Kin
devoted and caring
My soulmate, my friend:
in confidence sharing

Sharing our secrets
our joys and sorrows
Sharing our dreams
and all our tomorrows

My Sister, my Kin
devoted and true
When I look in the mirror
I think of you.

CATEGORY: **SISTER**   TITLE: **MY SISTER, MY KIN**

FITS 8 X 10 FRAME | FOR FUTURE USE, A PRINTABLE PDF CAN BE PURCHASED AT **PDFCALLIGRAPHY.COM**

My Sister, my twin
devoted and caring
My soulmate, my friend
in confidence sharing

Sharing our secrets
our joys and sorrows
Sharing our dreams
and all our tomorrows

My Sister, my twin
devoted and true
When I look in the mirror
I think of you.

CATEGORY: **SISTER**   TITLE: **MY SISTER, MY TWIN**

FITS 8 X 10 FRAME | FOR FUTURE USE, A PRINTABLE PDF CAN BE PURCHASED AT **PDFCALLIGRAPHY.COM**

Sister-in-law

Time only endears
 it cannot fade—
The memories
 that we have made.

Through quiet waters
 or stormy weather
We have as friends
 been together.

And though we did not
 choose our fate—
We were put together
 by our choice of mates.

I'm glad to know
 someone like you.
A sister-in-law
 and best friend too.

CATEGORY: **SISTER**   TITLE: **MY SISTER-IN-LAW**

129

Sorority Sisters

We've shared so many good times;
we've even shared some tears.
We have a special friendship
that'll grow stronger through the years.
Even though we're not really sisters,
we knew from the very start...
We were put together in college
to be sisters in our hearts.

~Mary Kay Brewster

PDFCalligraphy.com

Son

All the years that I've known you you've been so inclined
To be different and daring; to be one of a kind.
You've never been afraid to go it alone.
You have strength and courage and a mind of your own.

You demonstrate confidence no matter the test,
And I've never seen you give less than your best.
I'm proud of the wisdom and lesson you've learned
That respect from others can only be earned.

Your strong wit and humor are also a part
Of making us happy and touching my heart.
Your caring and sharing and love combined
Work together, my son, to make you one of a kind

PDFCalligraphy.com

Mary Lou Brewster © '15

CUT ALONG DOTTED LINE

CATEGORY: **SON**   TITLE: **SON**

FITS 8 X 10 FRAME | FOR FUTURE USE, A PRINTABLE PDF CAN BE PURCHASED AT **PDFCALLIGRAPHY.COM**   131

What Can We Give To Him

What can we give to Him, in service for the King?
What can we give to Him? Our lives, an offering.

As we become as one, our hearts together seed.
As we have just begun, our will is His to lead.
In God we will entrust, our home to give to Him.
As He has first loved us; with love we will begin.

When life is hard to bear, the path is hard to see;
we give our burdens there, to Christ at Calvary.
His word we will obey. The cross we will defend.
No matter come what may, He's closer than a friend.

Our talents are from Him. Our time is not our own.
He giveth all of them. These gifts are His alone.
As we together vow to live our lives for Him;
so we together bow in praise to worship Him.

What can we give to Him in service for the King?
What can we give to Him? Our lives, an offering.

Mary Kay & Kevin Brewster

PDFCalligraphy.com

CUT ALONG DOTTED LINE

TWO HEARTS

ONE LOVE

Two hearts we have
that beat as one
Our life together
has just begun

Soulmates we are
best friends we'll be
We'll share our joys
through eternity

We'll build our home
with help from above
We have two hearts
we share one love

CATEGORY: **WEDDING**   TITLE: **TWO HEARTS, ONE LOVE** (can be personalized)

FITS 8 X 10 FRAME | FOR FUTURE USE, A PRINTABLE PDF CAN BE PURCHASED AT **PDFCALLIGRAPHY.COM**

Two hearts, once joined in friendship, united now with love.

MQO '96

PDFCalligraphy.com

CATEGORY: **WEDDING**   TITLE: **TWO HEARTS, ONCE JOINED** (can be personalized)

FITS 8 X 10 FRAME | FOR FUTURE USE, A PRINTABLE PDF CAN BE PURCHASED AT **PDFCALLIGRAPHY.COM**

The greatest
of these is
LOVE 1 COR 13:1-13

Love . . . is patient and kind
it is not jealous, or conceited, or
proud, or provoked; love does not
keep a record of wrongs; love is
not happy with evil, but is
pleased with the truth.
Love never gives up; its
faith, hope and patience
never fail.

PDFCalligraphy.com

CATEGORY: **WEDDING**   TITLE: **THE GREATEST OF THESE** (can be personalized)

FITS 8 X 10 FRAME | FOR FUTURE USE, A PRINTABLE PDF CAN BE PURCHASED AT **PDFCALLIGRAPHY.COM**

Grandma

You've always been there, Grandma,
  to soothe and to confide.
It seems no matter what,
  you were always by my side.

I'm glad that you are here with me
  on this special day.
You give me so much comfort
  in oh so many ways.

Thank you for your wisdom
  and all your loving care.
I hope you know I realize
  a Grandma's love is rare.

Yes, you have always been there
  showing confidence and pride.
And even as I marry,
  I feel your love inside.

- Mary Kay Brewster

PDFCalligraphy.com

CATEGORY: **WEDDING**   TITLE: **GRANDMA - YOU'VE ALWAYS**

If there could be a shining rainbow
that reaches from your heart to mine,
the pot of gold at either end
could never buy your love so fine.

If there could be a soaring mountain
with height that reaches to the sun,
it could never be too high to climb
to prove the love we have begun.

If there could be a spanning ocean
with depth that reaches to unknown,
it could never match the depth of love
that grows within this heart you've shown.

If there could be a lowly valley
with warmth that radiates from sun,
its warmth could never match my warmth
from knowing you're my only one.

Mary Kay Brewster

PDFCalligraphy.com

On This Your Wedding Day

On this your special wedding day
as you celebrate your love,
the angels are rejoicing
from the celestial realms above.
The years will seem to blend into one
as your love endures time's test.
Each day will seem like you've just begun
when you give each other your best.
Your love will last eternally
as you vow to become one.
You'll cherish this day forever
and anticipate memories to come.
The years will only seem like days,
and the days like only minutes.
The vows you promise each other today
is the moment you begin it.
So, cherish the love you've shared so far
and anticipate memories to come.
For your love will last forever
as your hearts entwine as one.

Mary Kay Brewster

PDFCalligraphy.com

CATEGORY: **WEDDING**   TITLE: **ON THIS YOUR**

FITS 8 X 10 FRAME | FOR FUTURE USE, A PRINTABLE PDF CAN BE PURCHASED AT **PDFCALLIGRAPHY.COM**   138

Only One Chance

Have you ever stopped to wonder
when you came into the world;
That moment of conception
when you started to unfurl?
He spoke you into being;
a moment so sublime.
God planned for your existence
from the very beginning of time.
You only had one chance at life;
only one chance to be you.
And when you were conceived
it was only God who knew.
What right does any man have
to decide the life of another?
What happened to the reverence of life
for our sisters and our brothers?

Millions have been aborted
because of the selfishness of man.
No one can convince me
that this is what God planned.
So I ask you to think back
when your mother pondered you.
Was it an inconvenient time?
Did she wonder what to do?
There should never be a question;
whether to keep or do away.
For when a life is terminated
it's a sad and awful day.
So reverence life and hold it dear,
cherish it with all your might.
Each and every baby deserves
their rightful chance at life.

~ Mary Kay Brewster

PDFCalligraphy.com

CATEGORY: **RIGHT TO LIFE**   TITLE: **ONLY ONE CHANCE**

FITS 8 X 10 FRAME | FOR FUTURE USE, A PRINTABLE PDF CAN BE PURCHASED AT **PDFCALLIGRAPHY.COM**   139

No Choice

I'm writing you, dear Mother. I hope you long for me.
I hope you think about me and wonder who I'd be.
Please don't forget about me even though your heart may break.
Just ask for God's forgiveness and learn from your mistake.

Perhaps you didn't realize as you acted out of fear,
and took my life that fateful day, my voice you'd someday hear.
You acted one brief moment, thinking you would find relief.
But instead, you traded my life for feelings of regret and grief.

I had no voice; I had no choice. You took my life from me.
I hope you see your choice was wrong and get down on your knees.
I hope I didn't die in vain. Let others learn from you,
that a baby in a mother's womb are precious people too.

I never got the chance to feel the sun upon my face,
or feel the grass between my toes while to your arms I race.
Who knows what great accomplishments; what goals would I've achieved?
And think of all the care and love we both could have received.

And though I never had a chance to be born on earth below,
I'm a child up here in heaven: oh, what love God does bestow.
So, don't think of me as gone away; my journey's just begun.
I'm living up in heaven now with my Father and His Son.

Mary Kay Brewster

PDFCalligraphy.com

CATEGORY: **RIGHT TO LIFE**   TITLE: **NO CHOICE**

Your Name

What comes to mind when your name is heard?
What thoughts are thought in such a word?
Do people say your name in praise,
or does it cause eyebrows to raise?

We love to have our name adored.
Reproach and shame we can't afford.
The way we act could bring disgrace,
so be careful what you do or say.

Your name is given for you to treasure,
and often by it you are measured.
With all your actions, words, and deeds,
you're sure to plant everlasting seeds.

So, protect and guard the name you bear
like a precious jewel, rich and rare.
And when your name is spoken in pride,
you'll be glad that you don't have to hide.

Mary Kay Brewster

PDFCalligraphy.com

CUT ALONG DOTTED LINE

CATEGORY: **MISCELLANEOUS**   TITLE: **YOUR NAME**

FITS 8 X 10 FRAME | FOR FUTURE USE, A PRINTABLE PDF CAN BE PURCHASED AT **PDFCALLIGRAPHY.COM**

No Voice

One day I turned around. I found my life had changed.
The family that I knew so well was suddenly rearranged.
No longer did my mom and dad desire to live this way.
Without even consulting me, my dad just left one day.

Eventually I went to live with dad and his new wife.
Again, I had no choice or say about my brand-new life.
When adults mess up and boggle things, the children have no choice.
They're left to deal with doubt and pain; in short, they have no voice.

Then one day, they will wake up and suddenly realize
the road of life is not so smooth, but not to their surprise.
They'll realize that the choices of others are not the ones they'll make.

They'll take a look at mom and dad and learn from their mistakes.
So even if you're dealt a hand that doesn't go your way,
make the best of what you have and go take on the day!

Mary Kay Brewster

PDFCalligraphy.com

God is Looking for Worshipers

God is looking for worshipers. God is looking for worshipers.
Clap you hands. Move your feet. Raise your hands in praise to Him.
Dance for Him. Praise His name. Pray to Him in Jesus' Name.

His eyes are roaming the earth to see who exalts him throughout the week.
Share His word. Win the lost. Bless the poor at any cost.
Show His love through your deeds.
Thank Him daily for all your needs.

God is looking to bless your life. Worship Him with all your might.
Sing to Him. Lift your praise. Sing a song of His amazing grace.
Harmonize with your voice. Sing it out. Let's all rejoice.

God is looking for faithfulness. He desires your fellowship.
He invites you to His throne today. Receive His Power in a mighty way.
Sit with Him. Commune with Him. He'll be with you throughout the day.

God is looking to be your friend. He invites you to dwell with Him.
Thank Him for your trials each day. In them, He will help you find a way.
Share with Him your inmost thoughts, though He already knows your heart.
God is looking for worshipers!

Mary Kay Brewster

PDFCalligraphy.com

CATEGORY: **HEAVEN INSPIRED**   TITLE: **GOD IS LOOKING FOR WORSHIPERS**
FITS 8 X 10 FRAME | FOR FUTURE USE, A PRINTABLE PDF CAN BE PURCHASED AT **PDFCALLIGRAPHY.COM**   143

All Things Work Together

Are you weary in well doing; your strength not sufficient?
Let His arms everlasting uphold you.
Does your faith ever waiver; your hope fade away?
Look to Him; Let His strength be your stay.

For all things work together for good, to them
who love Him and keep His commandments.

_____

Has humility turned to pride; your love, turned to strife?
Let the Lord take control of your life.
Can you fall on your knees and call on the Savior?
Let your words of compassion find favor.

For all things work together for good to them
who love Him and keep His commandments.

_____

Are you walking in darkness; no light from this world?
Let the Lord shed light from His Word.
Are you searching for meaning this world cannot offer?
Look to Jesus; in Him you will prosper.

For all things work together for good to them
who love Him and keep His commandments.

Mary Kay Brewster

PDFCalligraphy.com

CATEGORY: **HEAVEN INSPIRED**   TITLE: **ALL THINGS WORK TOGETHER**

FITS 8 X 10 FRAME | FOR FUTURE USE, A PRINTABLE PDF CAN BE PURCHASED AT **PDFCALLIGRAPHY.COM**   144

Song of Blessing

May the Lord bless you and keep you and cause his face to shine on you,
and give you amazing grace.

May the Lord let the light of his countenance shine on you
and give you peace and give you the power of blessing.

May He fill you with His love each day, and may His Word astound you.
May His blessings give you power to face trials all around you.

May you bless others as you've been blessed.
Find it in your heart to bless, even those who've cursed you and used you.

When you bless others, you will be blessed.
He will fill you with his righteousness, and you will find the power of blessing.

May He fill you with His love each day, and may His Word astound you.
May His blessings give you power to face trials all around you.

May God's best intentions shine on your life; release you from all fear and strife.
May you truly find the power of blessing.

The power of life and death are in the tongue; speak words of kindness,
words of love, and you will have the power of blessing.

May He fill you with His love each day, and may His Word astound you.
May His blessings give you power to face trials all around you.

Mary Kay Brewster

PDFCalligraphy.com

CATEGORY: **HEAVEN INSPIRED** TITLE: **SONG OF BLESSING**

Declaration Song

Open the Heavens, rain down your love.
Pour out your Spirit, descend like a dove.

Endow me with power. Fill me with grace.
Your mercies are new with each morning I face.

Make me a blessing so others can see
Your power and glory are living in me.

Your throne room I long for, nothing compares
to the promise of heaven and the treasure it shares.

Come now and hasten Your soon return.
Catch me up Jesus, I lay down my crown.

Make me a blessing so others can see
Your power and glory are living in me.

I'll get out of the way Lord, let You take control.
You'll be my pilot, I won't go alone.

God the eternal, my refuge is He;
Life everlasting, His promises I seek.

Make me a blessing so others can see
Your power and glory are living in me.

Make me a vessel Lord, fit for the King.
Give me a message, Your praises I sing.

Mary Kay Brewster

PDFCalligraphy.com

Heaven On Earth

You can have Heaven on earth when you walk in His way.
Accept Jesus in your heart and learn how to pray.,
Follow His Word. Treat others with love,
Surrender your life. Get grace from above.

This is the way, Walk ye in it.
God will be there when you begin it.
Grow closer to Him with each new day.
Have Heaven on earth, when you walk in His way.

Grow in God. Be accountable.
Be filled with His love; love insurmountable.
Pray, "Grow me Lord. Help me follow Your way.
Use me where You're working today."

This is the way, Walk ye in it.
God will be there when you begin it.
Grow closer to Him with each new day.
Have Heaven on earth, when you walk in His way.

Show others His love. Bless those you see.
You will be blessed beyond belief.
Don't be afraid to show your faith.
Blessings are yours when you walk in His way.

This is the way. Walk ye in it.
God will be there when you begin it.
Grow closer to Him with each new day.
Have Heaven on earth when you walk in His way.

Mary Kay Brewster

PDFCalligraphy.com

CUT ALONG DOTTED LINE

CATEGORY: **HEAVEN INSPIRED** TITLE: **HEAVEN ON EARTH**

FITS 8 X 10 FRAME | FOR FUTURE USE, A PRINTABLE PDF CAN BE PURCHASED AT **PDFCALLIGRAPHY.COM**   147

Mold My Heart

I fold my hands next to my heart
and then I say a prayer.
Lord, lead me where You're working now.
How can You use me there?

I want to do Your will, oh Lord.
I give thanks with all my heart.
Please take my life and use me,
Lord. I want to do my part.

Lord, use my hands and mold my heart
to serve You every day.
May my hands work hard and my heart be tender
to the needs along the way.

Mary Kay Brewster

PDFCalligraphy.com

CATEGORY: **HEAVEN INSPIRED** TITLE: **MOLD MY HEART**

Let Go and Let God

I'm tired of life being a control game;
pulling strings to make things go my way.
It's time that I give in and let the Master win.
It's time for me to let Him have His way.

I got up this morn with great expectations;
thinking things were bound to go my way.
But one thing I forgot was to ask God what He thought.
And then my plans were crushed before my eyes.

I know now never to anticipate;
to count on things I try to manipulate.
For the calculated ways of man may not fit God's plan.
That is why I've learned to simply say.

Let go and let God have His way.
Let go and Let Him be your stay.
Let go and let God guide your day.
Let go and let God.

Mary Kay Brewster

PDFCalligraphy.com

CATEGORY: **HEAVEN INSPIRED** TITLE: **LET GO AND LET GOD**

Give Thanks In All Things

Have you ever stopped to wonder what God's will is for your life?
And do you wrestle with the flesh and have a lot of strife?
Don't look to self or others to find His perfect will,
unless you want to spend your life climbing up a hill.

It's easy to be thankful when blessings you receive.
But when a trial comes your way you struggle to believe
that God can work a miracle and turn your life around.
When praise and honor go to Him rich blessings will abound.

Slow down my friend and take a look, He's been there from the start.
It's in His word in black and white, just open up your heart.
He says, "Give thanks in all things." This is His will for you.
Thank Him for the blessings and tribulations too.

Mary Kay Brewster

PDFCalligraphy.com

God's Tear Bottle

God understands the language of tears;
whether we cry from joy or out of fear.
He puts my tears in a bottle for me.
He treasures them most when I'm down on my knees.

So give your tears to the Master above.
He'll bottle them up with His unfailing love.
Whether you're joyful, or happy, or fearful, or sad,
tears are a language God understands.

Mary Kay Brewster

PDFCalligraphy.com

The Question

Don't hesitate to ask Him, "Where are You working Lord?"
When you ask the question, the answer He'll afford.
Seek and you will find Him. Knock upon His door.
He will answer, "My child, rich blessings are in store."

Don't hesitate to ask Him, "What can I do for you?"
For when you ask the question, He'll show you what to do.
Serve the Lord with gladness. Come before His throne.
Unless you ask the question, you will not be shown.

My friend, have you stopped to ask Him, "Why did you die for me?"
He'll answer with compassion, "I came to set you free."
The most important question, "Will you come into my heart?"
Will free you from the chains of sin and give a fresh new start.

So, stop and ask the question; the answer you'll receive.
And when He gives the answer, you'll suddenly believe
that God can work a miracle and turn your life around.
For when you ask the question, rich blessings will abound.

Mary Kay Brewster

CATEGORY: **HEAVEN INSPIRED** TITLE: **THE QUESTION**

FITS 8 X 10 FRAME | FOR FUTURE USE, A PRINTABLE PDF CAN BE PURCHASED AT **PDFCALLIGRAPHY.COM**

Real Joy

You may not get your way at times;
in fact, you'll be annoyed.
But no matter what may come your way,
you can always have real joy.

There are times you won't be happy.
There are times you'll feel a void.
But no matter what your state may be,
you can always have real joy.

You won't always get the things you want;
whether wants or needs or toys.
But no matter what you want or need,
you can always have real joy.

The things of earth are tempting.
They are only Satan's ploy.
But no matter what he tempts you with,
you can always have real joy.
For joy is something that Jesus brings.
You must realize from the start;
joy is a gift that Jesus gives
when He comes into your heart.

Mary Kay Brewster

PDFCalligraphy.com

A Broken Heart

Two nails were driven through His hands.
His side was pierced and torn.
His feet were bound with a single nail.
He wore a crown of thorns.

"My Father," He cried, "Forgive them.
They know not what they do."
They could not break His spirit,
but His heart was broken in two.

No sins of His own to die for;
only our sins did He bear.
No life of His own did He cry for;
unselfish love so rich and rare.

He sacrificed every part of Himself;
not just part, but the whole.
His hands, His feet, His head, His side
were pierced and torn to save my soul.

I can only wonder how He felt.
In a cruel way they pierced each part.
His body was torn and wracked with pain,
yet the only thing broken was His heart.

Mary Kay Brewster

PDFCalligraphy.com

The Day
Before He Died

Think of how you'd feel if you knew you had to die
an undeserving death that was based on other people's lies.
Think of what you'd do if you knew you could get away.
Would you run or would you willingly stay?

He knew He had to die, but yet, He had a choice.
The angels would have come with one echo of His voice.
But yet, He chose to die to demonstrate His love,
so that someday we can be with Him above.

No sin He had to hide. No deed was left undone.
His Father spoke with pride, "Well done, My faithful Son"
And since He knew no sin, He knew that He would be
the perfect substitute on the cross of Calvary.

The day before He died, what was He thinking?
The day before He died, how did He feel?
Jesus stayed and paid the price,
A price He did not have to pay.
I'm so glad He chose to die that day.

Mary Kay Brewster

PDFCalligraphy.com

The Blanket of Blood

When I was a child I tried to hide
when I knew that I had done wrong.
I crawled under a blanket on top of my bed;
the wait seemed oh, so long.

Would Mom or Dad come and look for me
when they discovered what I had done?
Then the blanket was lifted and there they stood,
and there was no place to run.

"Forgive me," I begged, as I grabbed dad's leg,
"I know what I did was wrong."
"I forgive you," he said, "and God will too,
when to His fold you belong."

For you see one day the Savior
died to demonstrate His love.
His blood flowed down from the cross that day
and created a blanket of blood.

So, place your sins in His blanket;
His precious blanket of blood.
No more to be seen, no more to hide;
when your sins are covered by His blood.

Receive His blanket, His blanket of love.
Your sins He'll cover with His blanket of blood.
His love can heal you, and He'll forgive you,
when your sins are covered, covered by His blood.

Mary Kay Brewster

PDFCalligraphy.com

CATEGORY: **HEAVEN INSPIRED** TITLE: **THE BLANKET OF BLOOD**

FITS 8 X 10 FRAME | FOR FUTURE USE, A PRINTABLE PDF CAN BE PURCHASED AT **PDFCALLIGRAPHY.COM** 156

We All Bleed The Same

There I was scrolling, reading every post,
when I came across a catchy song that had a familiar boast.
"We all bleed the same." The lyrics were loud and clear.
It touched my heart and made me think of a subject oh so dear.

With all the hate and prejudice and debating whose lives matter,
I thought of the blood of Jesus through all the debate and clatter.
His blood is not the same as ours, it has a saving power;
the power to wash away our sins with each passing hour.

He was born in a lowly manger, the precious Son of God.
He only had one mission on earth; to shed His precious blood.
He was mocked and bruised and beaten, and nailed to a rugged tree.
His blood flowed down from the cross that day
as a promise to you and me.

He made a way to heaven for this lost and dying world;
a gift so freely given through the power of His blood.
So, when you hear the song "We All Bleed the Same",
Remember the blood of Jesus and call upon His Name.

Mary Kay Brewster

Who is the Ruler of Your Heart

Who is the ruler of your heart? Who influences all you do?
It's a question that must be answered. To thine own self be true.
"In the beginning was the Word, and the Word was with God,
and the Word was God." I ask, is this the path you trod?

For many reject His Word, this book we call the Bible.
Some think it has no power, as if it's a made up fable.
But I know His Word is alive. I hide it in my heart.
It's sharper than a two edged sword. It gave me a new start.

It tells me of the Savior; the One who came to die.
While I receive its promises, many say it is a lie.
And those who don't accept His Word don't realize, in part,
by default they chose a master that deceives their very heart.

He's called the prince of darkness, he comes to steal, kill and destroy.
He's got you where he wants you, stealing all your joy.
He's tempting you with worldly things, a temporary high;
causing you to think, for now, everything's all right.

After all, you're really not that bad, look at all the things you've done.
That's exactly where he wants you, and now he thinks he's won.
But I tell you friend, it's not too late to turn it all around.
Accept Christ as your Savior, rich blessings will abound.

Get power over the enemy. It's a promise from God's Son.
He gives you power and authority to defeat the evil one.
So now the question still remains. What answer will you impart?
Again, my friend I ask you, who's the ruler of your heart?

Mary Kay Brewster